Fall Rebus Writing

Combining Pictures and Print to Support Beginning Writers

Written by
Jo Fitzpatrick

Editors: Sheri Rous and Carla Hamaguchi
Illustrators: Darcy Tom and Corina Chien
Designer: Moonhee Pak
Cover Designer: Barbara Peterson
Art Director: Tom Cochrane
Project Director: Carolea Williams

Table of Contents

DIRECTED ACTIVITIES	Intro	Bears	Pumpkins	Bats	Spiders	Indians	Pilgrims
Picture Dictionary	13	27	44	61	78	95	112
Word Hunt	14	29	46	63	80	97	114
Secret Sentence Booklet	15	30	47	64	81	98	115
Bubble Writing	16	32	49	66	83	100	117
Connect a Sentence	17	33	50	67	84	101	118
Sentence Squares	18	34	51	68	85	102	119
Sentence/Story Builder	19	35	52	69	86	103	120
Story Box	20	36	53	70	87	104	121
Backward Story	21	37	54	71	88	105	122

INDEPENDENT/CENTER ACTIVITIES	Intro	Bears	Pumpkins	Bats	Spiders	Indians	Pilgrims
Descriptive Story	22	38	55	72	89	106	123
Shape Book	23	39	56	73	90	107	124
Class Book	24	41	58	75	92	109	126
Sequence Story	25	42	59	76	93	110	127

Introduction

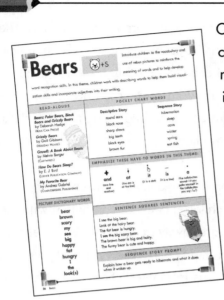

Children are born with the innate desire to communicate. In the early years, they label, mimic, and experiment with language. As they develop and grow, there is a natural tendency for them to expand their love of language into written expression; first through random scribbles and symbols, and then with specific words and sentences. Yet, when many of these children come to school, they are expected to use formal writing before they are ready. When children do not yet possess the prerequisites for writing, they may become frustrated and discouraged and may have the desire to give up trying to write.

Successful writing requires four key elements:

- the desire to say something
- the vocabulary to say it
- the ability to make words
- the structure with which to say it

As young children are acquiring these prerequisites, they need support and direction. It is important to be able to determine each child's developmental level and provide activities that will serve as building blocks to help children internalize the writing process.

Rebuses are a great way to provide children with the tools they need in order to learn to write. Rebuses are a wonderful way of combining pictures and print. Children quickly learn that words are meant to convey meaning. The use of rebuses exposes children to words that are above their reading level but part of their spoken vocabulary. As young children work with rebuses, they begin to understand the reading process and how decoding and encoding work. They also develop strong print awareness and utilize their own written language to practice their emerging reading skills. With the support of rebus vocabulary, beginning writers are empowered with the tools they need to express themselves in print.

The rebuses used throughout the program presented in Rebus Writing are designed to teach word meaning, expand vocabulary, and provide orthographic support. The rebuses incorporate pictures and phonetic units. By having to combine the elements in the picture, children are actually sounding out the rebus and developing their decoding and encoding skills.

Rebus Writing features seasonal themes that integrate content learning and writing. The integrated themes include science, social studies, and seasonal concepts. Each theme introduces related vocabulary, the printed word, and a pictorial rebus to teach children about the concept and provide the words they need to write sentences and related stories. Additionally, since many of the rebus activities are based on beginning reading skills, these activities can be incorporated into reading instruction.

The rebus vocabulary and themes start out very simple. This allows children to immediately recognize a specific word and its meaning. As children become competent with the rebus format, the vocabulary and rebuses become more involved. Children experiencing rebus for the first time may respond differently than their peers. The youngest children, when asked to write, may only copy the vocabulary words from the dictionary. Other children may add the rebus pictures for the words they write. The rebus pictures are very simple so that children can readily reproduce them. Children draw the rebus to reinforce the meaning of each word and to guarantee that they can accurately read what they wrote. As children gain confidence, they begin to combine words and write sentences.

At the beginning, emphasis is placed on adjectives so that children can develop their descriptive writing skills—a sentence with describing words or a descriptive story. As the themes progress, nouns, adjectives, and verbs are all used so that children can learn about word functions and expand beyond pattern sentences. The rebus vocabulary, in conjunction with related shared reading and "read aloud" books, gives children the background they need to formulate ideas and facilitate informational writing.

Beginning with the first theme, children cut and paste the rebus vocabulary into a picture dictionary. This provides each child with a "reference book" to use as he or she completes related activities and writes about the theme. Additionally, this vocabulary can be used for phonemic awareness and phonetic development. Use the reproducibles to help children practice the writing process. The multileveled activities will help you meet the needs of children at various writing stages. As a result, all children learn the same content but write about it at their own developmental level.

Providing the building blocks of writing has never been easier!

Using Rebus Writing to Differentiate

Learning to write is a developmental process that involves movement through designated writing stages. In order to develop stronger writing skills and move through these levels, children need to understand the writing process and how to express and organize ideas before putting them into print. For many, this is not an automatic or a natural process. Children need guidance and practice before they can easily turn oral language into written language.

To meet the needs of your children, complete the activities as a whole group, in small groups, or independently. They can be done orally with younger writers or collaboratively by writing on an enlarged reproducible page. Or, invite children to work with a partner to create sentences or stories. The independent or center activities include an art project and additional vocabulary. You can easily differentiate the activities to help children work at their own ability level. Use the follow-up activities for more advanced writers.

The activities in *Rebus Writing* are designed to give support to children at each and every beginning writing stage. The developmental activities for each theme use the rebus vocabulary to help children develop and expand their ideas. The activities involve individual student writing using support vocabulary; a Rebus Dictionary, pocket chart words, and related word webs are included in each theme. The level of difficulty can be adjusted to the needs and competency of the children and can range from sentence writing to story development. Beginning writers will become familiar with words and their meaning, while more advanced writers will be able to practice their spelling. Children will gain experience with different writing types: descriptive, narrative, and informational. Emphasis is placed on the following skills:

- sentence formation
- elaboration and expansion of ideas
- cloze completion
- sequence of events
- application of content

Children, no matter their ability level, will have access to the same content and information. They will be able to rely on their skill, interest, and readiness levels to apply this information. Adjust or tier the difficulty and focus of the activities (i.e., producing words, sentences, or stories) to differentiate the instruction based upon developmental needs.

The Rebus Approach provides built-in differentiation. Due to the nature of the program, children are able to use content to become self-improving writers. Young writers take and use the rebus and support activities at "face value" and learn how to use and combine words to develop meaningful sentences. Early writers use the support system to learn how to expand and elaborate ideas and develop related stories. More advanced writers use the Rebus Approach as a springboard to expand the informational content in their writing and to experiment with different writing genres. No matter the writing stage, the Rebus Approach empowers all children to become highly motivated and productive writers.

It is easy to address each child's developmental level. With exposure and practice, children will progress, at their own pace, from simple word writing to sentence and story writing. The activities included in each theme can be adapted accordingly. They can be done orally, as an interactive lesson, or independently for more advanced writers. The scope of the activities ranges from simple to more complex and can be used accordingly with children at various writing stages.

Getting Started

Initially, the rebuses might seem a little overwhelming to you, especially when looking at them in their entirety. However, it is important to remember that children learn the rebuses as they go. As they learn them, so do you. After a while, the graphics become second nature and you will begin to think in terms of rebuses! Use the following steps to make each child's rebus writing experience more memorable.

STEP 1
There are certain standard graphics that form the rebus vocabulary. It is important to be aware of these graphics and what they represent. Review the **Graphics for Phonetic Elements** (page 10), the **Positional Vocabulary** (page 11), and the **Everyday Rebuses** (page 12) to help you internalize the basic graphics that appear in the rebus vocabulary. You can also refer to these lists if you make rebuses for songs, charts, and other materials.

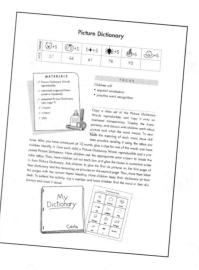

STEP 2
Prepare a **Picture Dictionary** for each child by either purchasing a 40-page, 8½" x 6⅞" (21.5 cm x 18 cm) composition book for each child or placing 40 pieces of blank paper into a folded piece of construction paper and stapling the left side. Write each child's name on the cover of the book. Make a few extra dictionaries in case a new child comes to class during the year. As children work in their dictionary, add the picture cards to the additional dictionaries.

STEP 3
Read aloud a **content-related book** that relates to the theme of study. This will provide children with some background knowledge and give them a chance to hear some of the theme words in context. A list of suggested literature selections is included on the section opener page for each theme of study. Continue reading additional theme-related books throughout the theme to help reinforce it.

STEP 4
Review the **section opener** page for the theme of study. This page provides information about the theme, a list of theme-related literature selections, a list of "Have-To Words," Sequence Story Pocket Chart Words, a Sequence Story Prompt, and Descriptive Story Pocket Chart Words.

STEP 5

As children write about the theme, they use many high-frequency words that are not in their Picture Dictionary. It is important that children spell these words correctly. If left to invented spelling and sounding out, errors will appear, be repeated, and then learned. **Have-To Words** are words that children have to learn to read and spell. These words have been incorporated into each theme and appear throughout the activities. Create a **Have-To Board** on a bulletin board. Write the Have-To Words from the unit of study on separate sentence strips, and attach the sentence strips to the bulletin board. Number the words, and place them in rows of up to five words. Add additional words from other classroom studies, as needed. Have children read and spell the words on the board. If a child needs assistance finding a word, tell the child to look in a specific row or give the child the number of the desired word. As children master each word, remove it from the board.

STEP 6

The **Directed Activities** section (pages 13–21) includes numerous activities and reproducibles that teach and reinforce the rebus words for each theme. Children practice their writing in a whole-class or small-group setting while gaining confidence in their skills.

STEP 7

The **Independent or Writing Center Activities** section (pages 22–25) provides even the youngest writer with an opportunity to use support vocabulary to process information, formulate ideas, and then put those ideas down on paper. The degree of difficulty can be adjusted from simple sentence writing to story development. In each theme, emphasis is placed on descriptive writing, informational writing, and sequential writing. A reproducible is included for each activity. Either have children work independently or in a writing center to complete the activities.

STEP 8

Activities rotate through the themes. For example, each theme has a Word Hunt activity. Read the activity directions (page 14) and use the **Rebus Page Number Box** at the top of each activity to find the accompanying reproducible for the theme you have chosen. For example, the Word Hunt reproducible for the Bears theme is on page 29.

THEME	🐻+S	🎃+S	b●+S	🕷+S	🧺+S	🎩+S
PAGE	29	46	63	80	97	114

Organizational Tips

Rebus Writing is an extensive resource for teachers of beginning writers. Differentiation and developmental instruction is built right into the program. Everything you need is here, including support materials, instructional word cards, and numerous activities.

All types of student grouping and instructional strategies can be used with the activities in this resource, depending on the range of ability levels in your classroom and your teaching style and preference. You can elect to complete the activities in whole-group, small-group, or independent settings. The following suggestions are made to serve as a springboard to help you design the best organizational plan that meets your children's particular needs.

WHOLE-GROUP INSTRUCTION

- Read-alouds
- Shared reading
- Have-To Words
- Introduction of rebus vocabulary
- Picture Dictionary
- Secret Sentence Booklets
- Bubble Writing
- Connect a Sentence

SMALL-GROUP (SKILL-BASED) INSTRUCTION

Group students according to their developmental needs for these activities:
- Sentence Squares
- Sentence/Story Builder
- Story Box
- Backward Story

SMALL-GROUP (HETEROGENEOUS) INSTRUCTION

Group students in small groups that consist of varied ability levels or as a center activity. Allow advanced students to work independently.
- Descriptive Story
- Shape Book
- Class Book
- Sequence Story

Basic Rebuses

The following graphics are used in many phonetic words to help children learn and apply the decoding process. These phonetic sounds are represented with a rebus that is related to the actual sound. Use the phrase to explain the rebus.

/th/   the stick-out-your-tongue sound

/sh/   the quiet sound

/ou/   the hammerhead sound
(what you say when you hit your finger with a hammer)

/oo/   the ghost sound

/ing/   the king of the *ing* sound

/ch/   the choo choo sound

/oo/   the muscle man sound
(what you say when you lift something heavy)

er^rrr **/er/**   hold onto the *r* (*ir* and *ur*)

/u/   the belly button sound—like when you poke yourself in the belly button
(this is used for the short u sound and the schwa sound)

"A" Note: if the rebus is in quotes, say the name of the letter—(for use with long vowel sounds). Use this when a letter name is a sound (i.e., /ar/ = "R" or candy = 🥫 + "D").

The following words use the above graphics. Once you get used to the phonetic graphics, you will see how easy it is to come up with rebuses for practically any word you want.

😛+"A"   "E"+🚂   r+👻+ m   😛+👑
they   **each**   **room**   **thing**

m+"A"+K   t+✋🔨+n   l+er^rrr+n   🤫+💪+d
make   **town**   **learn**   **should**

The following rebuses help describe locations. Write the rebuses on the board. As you introduce each rebus say the phrase so children will understand the graphic.

the dot is **in** the box

the dot is **out** of the box

the dot is **on** the box

the dot is **over** the box

the dot is **under** the box

the dot fell **from** the shelf

the dot is **between** the lines

the dot is **after** the line

the dot is **before** the line

the dot is **at** the line

the dot is at the **top** of the paper

the dot is at the **bottom** of the paper

The following rebuses are used for basic vocabulary. Write the rebuses on the board. Say each phrase when you introduce the rebus to children.

it **is** a line

it **is** a dot

pointing to **the** ___

it is **a** belly button

it's an **R** for the word are

it's a **saw**

that means **was**

this says **were**

one line **and** another

has—breathe out and say /s/

I **have** the dot

I **had** the dot but dropped it

one circle **with** another

will—/w/ + ill in bed

I **want** the dot

the car **went** down the street

do—/d/ + the ghost sound

the **don't** symbol

give me the box

I **gave** him the box

some—/s/ + belly button + /m/

I **did** it

didn't—did + /nt/

I **made** it with my hands

who—what an owl says

what's in the box

when—day or night

where in the world are you

why—the letter "y"

away—belly button + one way sign

Picture Dictionary

THEME	🐻+S	🎃+S	b♦+S	🕷+S	🪶+S	🎩+S
PAGE	27	44	61	78	95	112

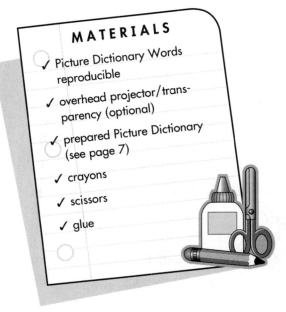

MATERIALS

- ✓ Picture Dictionary Words reproducible
- ✓ overhead projector/transparency (optional)
- ✓ prepared Picture Dictionary (see page 7)
- ✓ crayons
- ✓ scissors
- ✓ glue

FOCUS

Children will
- expand vocabulary.
- practice word recognition.

Copy a class set of the Picture Dictionary Words reproducible, and copy it onto an overhead transparency. Display the transparency, and discuss with children each rebus picture and what the word means. To reinforce the meaning of each word, have children practice reading it using the rebus pictures. After you have introduced all 12 words, give a clue for one of the words and have children identify it. Give each child a Picture Dictionary Words reproducible and a prepared Picture Dictionary. Have children use the appropriate color crayon to shade the color rebus. Then, have children cut out each box and glue the boxes in numerical order in their Picture Dictionary. Ask children to glue the first six pictures on the first page of their dictionary and the remaining six pictures on the second page. Then, have them label the pages with the correct theme heading. Have children keep their dictionary at their desk. To extend the activity, say a number and have children find the word in their dictionary and read it aloud.

Word Hunt

THEME	🐻+S	🎃+S	b●+S	🕷+S	🪶+S	🎩+S
PAGE	29	46	63	80	97	114

MATERIALS

✓ Word Hunt reproducible

✓ Picture Dictionaries
(see page 13)

FOCUS

Children will
• practice word recognition.
• use dictionary skills.

Have children point to each word for the theme of study in their Picture Dictionary as you say the word aloud. Give each child a Word Hunt reproducible. Point to the pictures on the reproducible. Explain to the class that they are to use their Picture Dictionary to locate the matching picture and write the corresponding word on the line underneath the picture on their reproducible. Tell children that at the bottom of the page they will discover a surprise sentence to complete. Point to the bracket and explain that this symbol means to start the sentence with a capital letter. Point to the dot at the end of the sentence. Explain that the dot represents a period and is at the end of a sentence. To extend the activity, write additional secret sentences on the board for children to complete. Note: Once children understand how to complete the activity, word practice may no longer be necessary.

Secret Sentence Booklet

THEME	🐻+S	🎃+S	b●+S	🕷+S	🧺+S	🎩+S
PAGE	30–31	47–48	64–65	81–82	98–99	115–116

MATERIALS

✓ Secret Sentence Booklet reproducibles

✓ scissors

✓ 5" x 11½" (12.5 cm x 21.5 cm) construction paper strips

✓ crayons or markers

✓ Picture Dictionaries (see page 13)

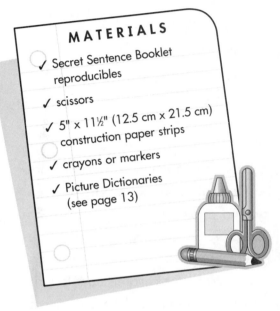

FOCUS

Children will

• expand vocabulary.

• write sentences.

Copy the Secret Sentence Booklet reproducibles for each child. Cut the reproducibles in half lengthwise on the line. Assemble them in numerical order. Staple the left side of a construction paper strip to the front and back of the reproducibles to make a booklet. Give each child a prepared Secret Sentence Booklet. Draw a rebus sentence (pictures only) from the reproducible on the board. Point to each rebus picture, and have children say the word that goes with the rebus. Next, write the word under the picture. Read the word for the picture. Emphasize to children that the word is written right under the picture to allow for space between words. Continue adding each remaining word under the correct rebus picture. Have children count the rebus pictures and words on the board. Ask them to open their Secret Sentence Booklet. Point to the bracket in the booklet and remind children that this symbol means to start the sentence with a capital letter. Have children trace each bracket with a green crayon or marker. Then, point to the dot at the end of each sentence and remind children that the dot represents a period and is the end of a sentence. Have children color each period with a red crayon or marker. Invite them to read the first rebus sentence in their booklet to discover what the Secret Sentence says. Have children use their Picture Dictionary to help them write each word under the appropriate picture. Have children complete one sentence in their booklet each day until they have completed all the sentences. Encourage them to read aloud their sentences.

Bubble Writing

MATERIALS

✓ Bubble Writing reproducible

✓ overhead projector/ transparency

✓ Picture Dictionaries (see page 13)

FOCUS

Children will
- practice word recognition.
- write sentences.

Copy a class set of the Bubble Writing reproducible. Copy it onto an overhead transparency, and display the transparency. Give each child a reproducible. Point to the pictures in the bubbles. Invite volunteers to "read" each rebus. Model for children how to write the words for the rebuses. Have children use their Picture Dictionary to help them write the correct word in each bubble. Explain to children that each blank in the sentence has a number that corresponds with the numbered bubbles. Show children how to use the numbered words in the bubbles to complete the numbered cloze sentences on the bottom of the page. Invite volunteers to read aloud the completed sentences.

Connect a Sentence

THEME	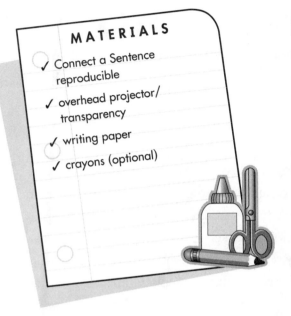+S	+S	b●+S	+S	+S	+S
PAGE	33	50	67	84	101	118

MATERIALS

✓ Connect a Sentence reproducible

✓ overhead projector/ transparency

✓ writing paper

✓ crayons (optional)

FOCUS

Children will
- write pattern sentences.
- expand rebus vocabulary.
- combine ideas.

Copy a class set of the Connect a Sentence reproducible. Copy it onto an overhead transparency, and display the transparency. Discuss the rebus pictures and their word meaning with the class. Give each child a reproducible. Have children combine the phrase in the center bubble with words from the connecting bubbles to create sentences and write them on a piece of paper. Explain to children that they need to choose words that make sense in a sentence. Ask if it makes sense to say *The bear looks funny and cute.* (yes) Ask if it makes sense to say *The bear looks big and little.* (no) Encourage children to combine words from more than one bubble to expand their sentences. To extend the activity, choose a word that appears in a bubble and have children trace the bubble with a given color crayon. Repeat this process with seven additional bubbles and crayons. Say a color or invite a volunteer to say a color, and have children read the center bubble and then add the word that appears in the corresponding color bubble. For example, if you say the color red, children read the center bubble and then finish the sentence with the text that appears in the red bubble (e.g., *The bear looks hungry.*)

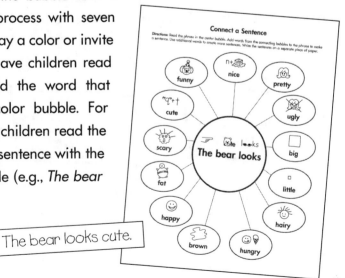

Sentence Squares

THEME	🐻+S	🎃+S	b♦+S	🕷+S	🪶+S	🎩+S
PAGE	34	51	68	85	102	119

MATERIALS

✓ Sentence Squares reproducible

✓ construction paper or card stock

✓ scissors

FOCUS

Children will practice sentence formation.

Copy a class set of the Sentence Squares reproducible onto construction paper or card stock for durability. Give each child a reproducible. Have children cut apart their squares. Say a short sentence that includes words from the reproducible. (Sample sentences are listed on the section opener page for the theme of study.) Have children select the appropriate word squares and arrange them in the correct order to make the sentence. Begin by saying the whole sentence, and then repeat the sentence a few words at a time as children find the squares to make that part of the sentence. Remind children that each sentence begins with a capital letter and ends with a punctuation mark. Repeat the process with additional sentences. To extend the activity, have children use their squares to make up their own sentences. As an option, send home the activity as homework, and have children bring back a list of the sentences they made.

Sentence/Story Builder

THEME	☺+S	🎃+S	b◆+S	🕷+S	🪶+S	🎩+S
PAGE	35	52	69	86	103	120

MATERIALS

✓ Sentence/Story Builder reproducible

✓ correction fluid (optional)

FOCUS

Children will develop a structured sentence or story.

Give each child a Sentence/Story Builder reproducible. Discuss the illustrations that describe *who, what, when, where,* and *why.* Help children use the illustrations to develop a sentence or story that includes these elements. Ask questions to help guide the sequence of the story and provide transition. For younger writers, concentrate on the composing process so children see how to connect ideas. For more advanced writers, help children formulate their ideas and model the writing process. When children are ready, have them complete the activity independently. To extend the activity, use correction fluid to delete the pictures and text from the "Is Doing What" and "Why" boxes. Have children add their own words and illustrations to these boxes and then write a story. Remind children that all sentences begin with a capital letter and end with a punctuation mark.

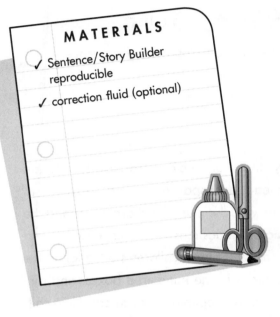

Story Box

THEME	🐻+S	🎃+S	b♦+S	🕷+S	🪶+S	🎩+S
PAGE	36	53	70	87	104	121

MATERIALS

- ✓ Story Box reproducible
- ✓ overhead transparency/ projector
- ✓ crayons (optional)

FOCUS

Children will develop a story sequence.

Copy the Story Box reproducible onto an overhead transparency, and display it. Discuss with the class the character(s) and the setting. Ask questions to help children expand their thinking. Direct children's attention to the illustrations in the numbered boxes, and discuss what is happening in each box. Help children use these three pictures to combine their ideas into a sequential story. Present the activity orally with emerging writers and as a guided writing lesson with more advanced writers. Ask children questions about the illustrations to help guide the sequence of events and provide transition. As children become more comfortable with these procedures, have them complete the activity independently. Provide a list of transition words (e.g., *once, first, then, next, finally, because*) to help them connect their ideas. To extend the activity, have more capable writers illustrate their own Story Box reproducible and write a story based upon the illustrations and picture sequence.

Backward Story

THEME	+S	+S	b +S	+S	+S	+S
PAGE	37	54	71	88	105	122

MATERIALS

✓ Backward Story reproducible

FOCUS

Children will understand story components and sequence.

Introduce the activity by reading aloud the end of the story as it appears on the Backward Story reproducible. Ask questions related to the story's ending to help children develop ideas for a beginning and middle. (Sample questions can be found on the reproducible.) Use the information gathered from the class discussion to help children orally organize a theme-related story with a beginning, middle, and ending. Have more advanced writers write their own story following a group discussion to gather and expand ideas. To extend the activity, have children come up with alternative story endings related to the theme. Divide the class into pairs, and have each pair of children complete a story based on the new ending.

Descriptive Story

THEME	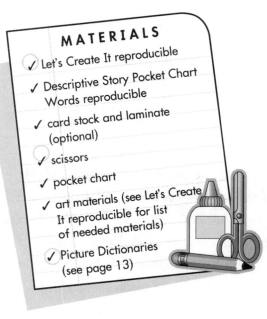 +S	+S	b +S	+S	+S	+S
PAGE	38	55	72	89	106	123

MATERIALS

- ✓ Let's Create It reproducible
- ✓ Descriptive Story Pocket Chart Words reproducible
- ✓ card stock and laminate (optional)
- ✓ scissors
- ✓ pocket chart
- ✓ art materials (see Let's Create It reproducible for list of needed materials)
- ✓ Picture Dictionaries (see page 13)

FOCUS

Children will use descriptive writing to write a sentence or story.

Make a copy of the Descriptive Story Pocket Chart Words from the page for the theme of study. As an option, copy the cards onto card stock and laminate them. Cut apart the word cards and place them in a pocket chart. Copy a class set of the Let's Create It reproducible. Create a completed art sample following the directions on the reproducible. Review the vocabulary in the Picture Dictionary for the theme, and introduce the word cards in the pocket chart. Show children the completed sample and review the steps they will need to follow to complete the project. Tell children that once they complete their project they are to write a sentence or story that goes with the project. Ask them to use the words from their Picture Dictionary and the word cards in the pocket chart to help them complete their writing. Have children work in a learning center to complete their project. When children have finished their project and writing, have them read their sentence or story to a partner or the whole class.

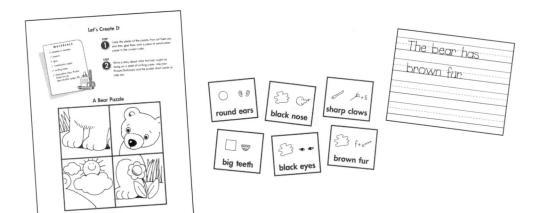

Shape Book

THEME	![bear +S]	![pumpkin +S]	b♦+S	![spider +S]	![basket +S]	![hat +S]
PAGE	39	56	73	90	107	124

MATERIALS

✓ Shape Book reproducible

✓ Word Web reproducible

✓ construction paper

✓ writing paper

✓ scissors

✓ stapler

✓ Picture Dictionaries (see page 13)

✓ crayons

FOCUS

Children will practice informational writing.

Copy one class set of the Shape Book reproducible on construction paper. Copy one class set of the Word Web reproducible. As an option, laminate the Word Web reproducible for durability and place it in a learning center. Create a sample Shape Book to share with the class. Staple writing paper between a Shape Book reproducible and a blank piece of construction paper to create a booklet for each child. Demonstrate for children how to cut out the shape cover and by doing so create shaped writing paper and a back cover at the same time.

Have children review the vocabulary words in their Picture Dictionary for the appropriate theme. Tell children that they are to write about something they have learned from their theme of study. Review the words that appear on the Word Web reproducible. Invite children to share ideas about what they will write about in their shape book. Encourage them to use descriptive words in their story. Have children use their Picture Dictionary and the Word Web reproducible to help them spell the words they need to write sentences or stories in their shape book.

Invite children to color the cover of their book once their story is completed. Place the reproducibles at a learning center, and have small groups of children complete their books in the center with an adult. Younger writers may just write simple pattern sentences, while more advanced writers will combine ideas and thoughts into simple stories. Invite children to read their sentences or story to a partner or to the class.

Class Book

THEME	🐻+S	🎃+S	b●+S	🕷+S	🪶+S	🎩+S
PAGE	41	58	75	92	109	126

MATERIALS

✓ Class Book reproducible

✓ construction paper

✓ Picture Dictionaries (see page 13)

✓ crayons or markers

✓ bookbinding materials

Children will use adjectives in a series.

Copy a class set of the Class Book reproducible. Use construction paper to make a front and back cover for the class book. Show children the cover and the reproducible. Explain to children that they will each complete a page for the class book. Tell them that the completed book will be on display so everyone will have a chance to see their "work in print" and read what their classmates wrote. Discuss the cloze activity on the reproducible, and emphasize that children will complete the sentences by using words from their Picture Dictionary and words that appear around the room. Have children complete the cloze activity at a learning center or independently. Encourage them to use their Picture Dictionary for ideas. Have an adult do the actual writing for younger children. Tell these children to read back the sentence after an adult writes it. Have children illustrate their sentence. Assemble the completed pages, add the cover to the book, and then read the book to the class. Display the book in a prominent place, and invite children to read it during free time.

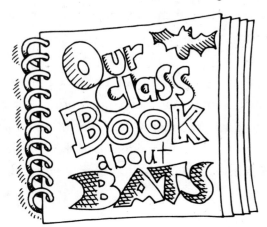

Sequence Story

THEME	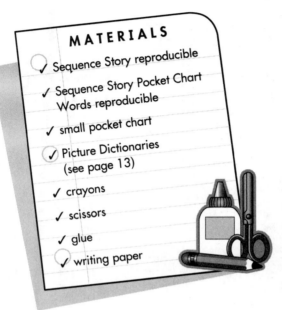+S	+S	b◆+S	+S	+S	+S
PAGE	42	59	76	93	110	127

MATERIALS

- ✓ Sequence Story reproducible
- ✓ Sequence Story Pocket Chart Words reproducible
- ✓ small pocket chart
- ✓ Picture Dictionaries (see page 13)
- ✓ crayons
- ✓ scissors
- ✓ glue
- ✓ writing paper

FOCUS

Children will write about a sequence of events over time.

Copy a class set of the Sequence Story reproducible. Create a sample Sequence Story to share when introducing the lesson. Make a copy of the Sequence Story Pocket Chart Words reproducible. Cut apart the word cards, and place them in a small pocket chart. Share these words with the class. Have them also review the words in their Picture Dictionary for the appropriate theme. Discuss with children the Sequence Story Prompt, which is listed on the section opener page. Show the class your Sequence Story sample. Explain to them that they will receive a series of pictures to color, cut out, and glue in proper sequence. Use the pictures from your sample as you discuss the sequence. Give each child a Sequence Story reproducible. Tell children to color, cut out, and glue the pictures in order on their reproducible. Then, have children use the Sequence Story Prompt to help them write a story about the theme on a piece of writing paper. Encourage children to use their Picture Dictionary and the pocket chart words to help them spell the words they need in order to write their sequence story. Invite volunteers to share their completed story.

Bears

🐻 + s

Introduce children to the vocabulary and use of rebus pictures to reinforce the meaning of words and to help develop word recognition skills. In this theme, children work with describing words to help them build visualization skills and incorporate adjectives into their writing.

READ-ALOUDS

Bears: Polar Bears, Black Bears and Grizzly Bears
by Deborah Hodge
(KIDS CAN PRESS)

Grizzly Bears
by Gail Gibbons
(HOLIDAY HOUSE)

Growl!: A Book About Bears
by Melvin Berger
(CARTWHEEL)

How Do Bears Sleep?
by E. J. Bird
(LERNER PUBLICATION COMPANY)

My Favorite Bear
by Andrea Gabriel
(CHARLESBRIDGE PUBLISHING)

PICTURE DICTIONARY WORDS

bear
brown
scary
my
see
big
happy
fat
hungry
I
the
look(s)

POCKET CHART WORDS

Descriptive Story	Sequence Story
round ears	hibernation
black nose	sleep
sharp claws	cave
big teeth	winter
black eyes	spring
brown fur	eat fish

EMPHASIZE THESE HAVE-TO WORDS IN THIS THEME:

+
and
(one line and another)

at
(the dot is at the line)

it
(it is a dot)

—
is
(it is a line)

a
(the bellybutton sound—if you poke yourself in the bellybutton you say /u/)

SENTENCE SQUARES SENTENCES

I see the big bear.
Look at the hairy bear.
The fat bear is hungry.
I see the big scary bear.
The brown bear is big and hairy.
The funny bear is cute and happy.

SEQUENCE STORY PROMPT

Explain how a bear gets ready to hibernate and what it does when it wakes up.

Picture Dictionary Words

Directions: Read each word. Cut out the picture cards and glue them in your Picture Dictionary.

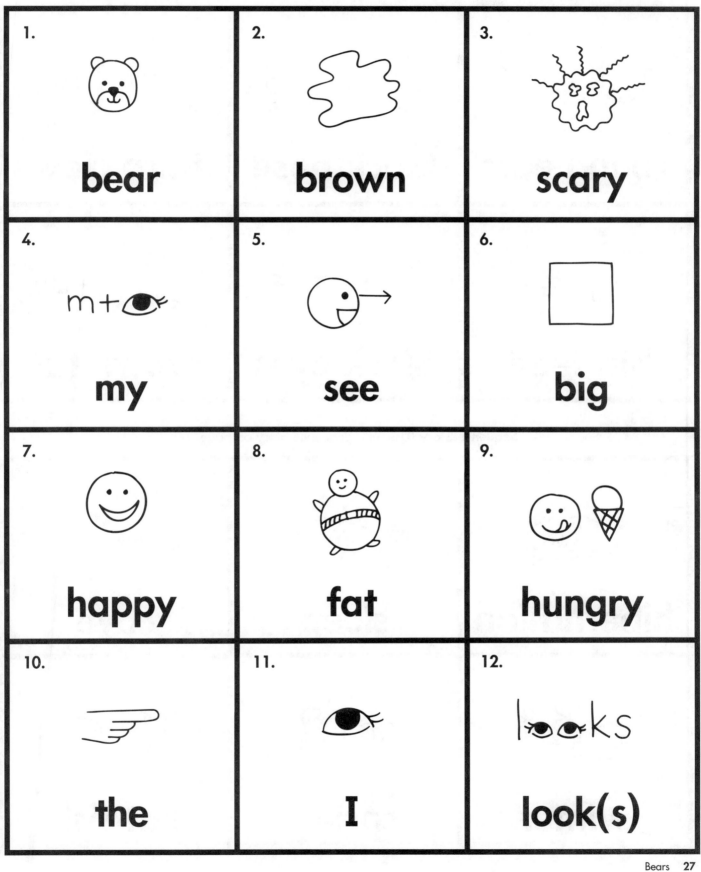

1. bear

2. brown

3. scary

4. my

5. see

6. big

7. happy

8. fat

9. hungry

10. the

11. I

12. look(s)

Pocket Chart Words

Descriptive Story (Use with Let's Create It on page 38)

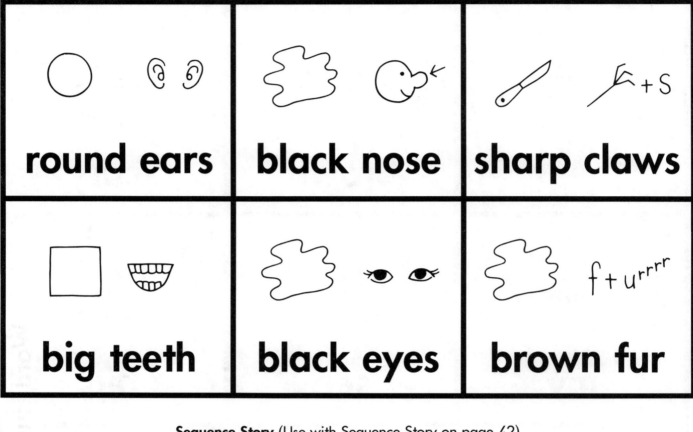

| round ears | black nose | sharp claws |
| big teeth | black eyes | brown fur |

Sequence Story (Use with Sequence Story on page 42)

| hibernation | sleep | cave |
| winter | spring | eat fish |

Rebus Writing • Fall © 2004 Creative Teaching Press

Name _____

Word Hunt

Directions: Use your Picture Dictionary to help you find the word that goes with each picture. Write the correct word below each picture. Complete the special sentence at the bottom of the page.

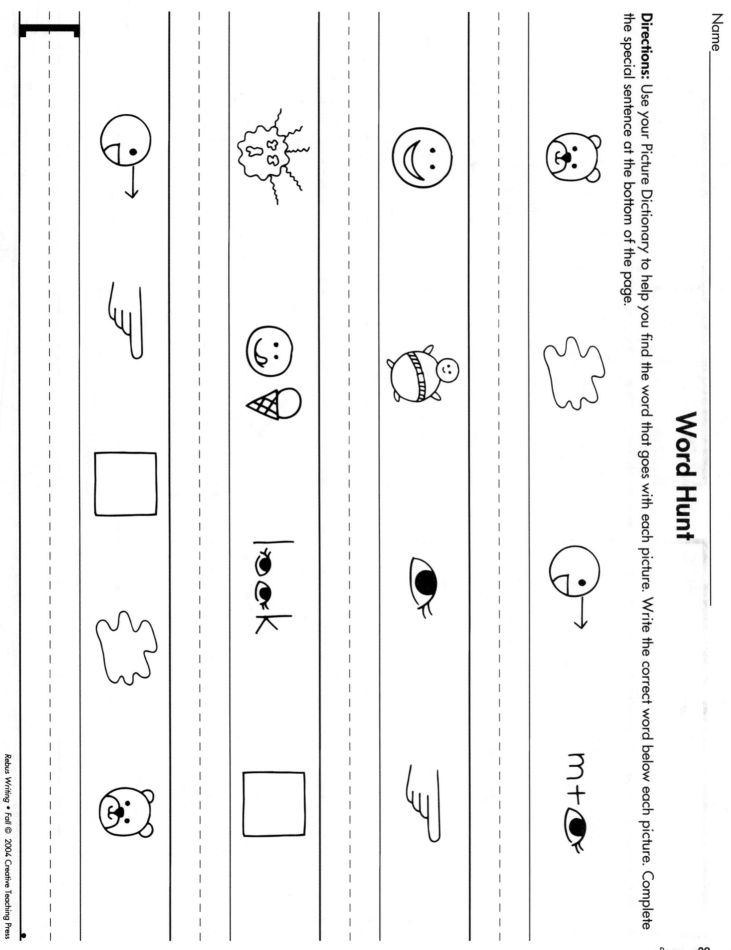

Rebus Writing • Fall © 2004 Creative Teaching Press

Secret Sentence Booklet

Directions: Write the correct word under each rebus picture.

1

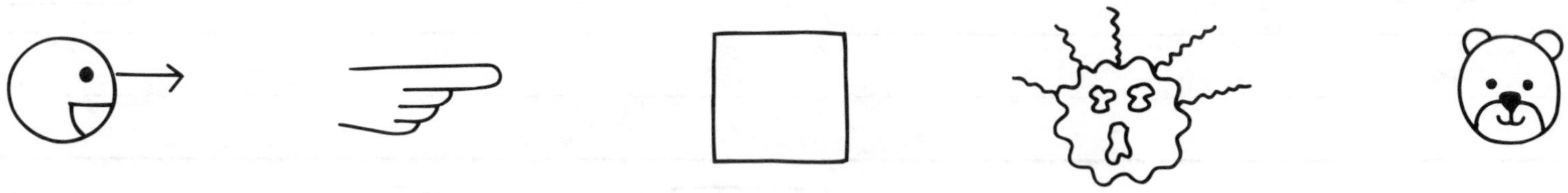

2

Rebus Writing • Fall • © 2004 Creative Teaching Press

Secret Sentence Booklet

Directions: Write the correct word under each rebus picture.

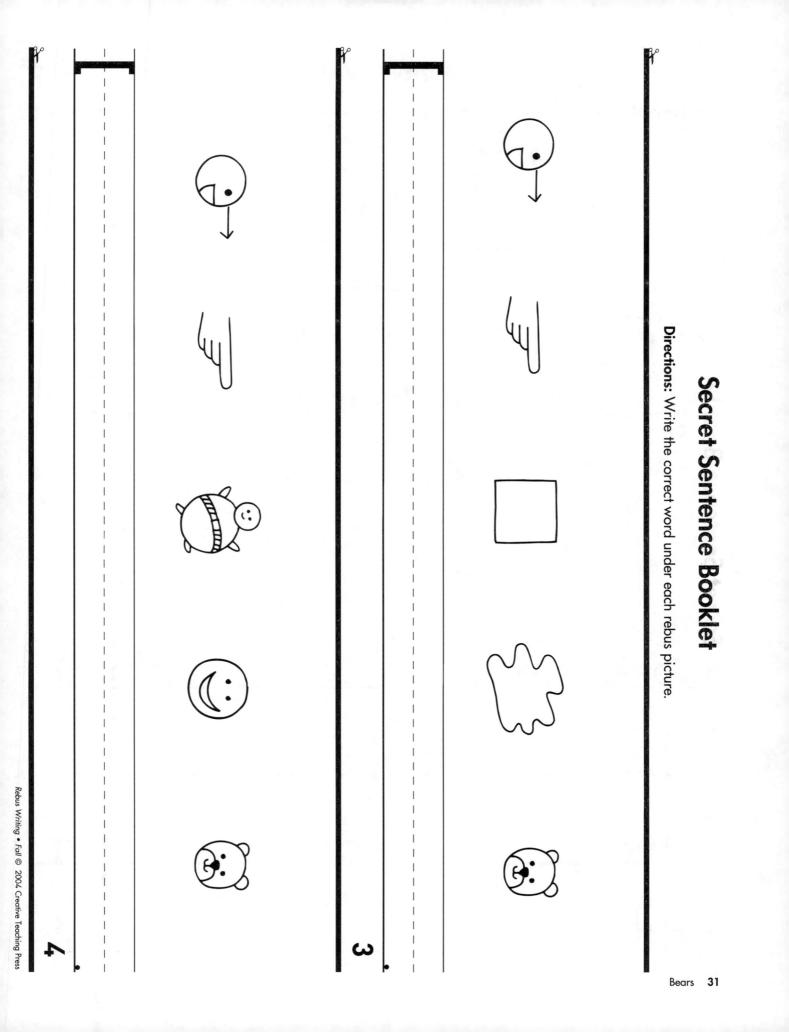

3

4

Name_____

Bubble Writing

Directions: Write the correct word in each bubble. Use these words to complete the sentences at the bottom of the page.

I See the _____ _____ bear.

The bear looks _____.

The _____ bear is _____

and _____.

Rebus Writing • Fall © 2004 Creative Teaching Press

Connect a Sentence

Directions: Read the phrase in the center bubble. Add words from the connecting bubbles to the phrase to make a sentence. Use additional words to create more sentences. Write the sentences on a separate piece of paper.

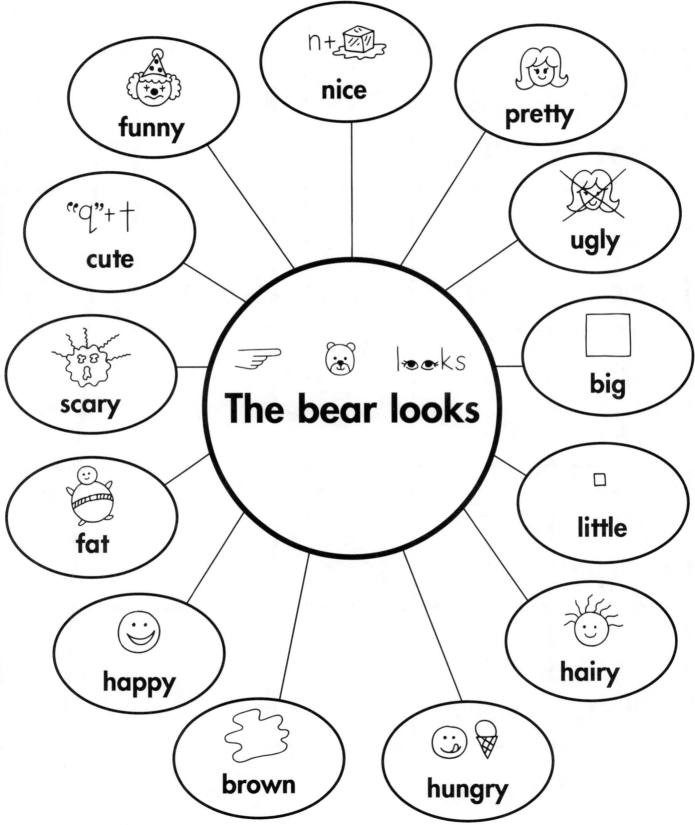

Sentence Squares

Directions: Read the word cards. Cut apart the cards and mix them up. Make sure that the words are face up. Use the word cards to make sentences.

fat	and	the	see	funny
Look	at	bear	brown	pretty
I	cute	big	hairy	is
hungry	little	scary	He	.
happy	The			

Rebus Writing • Fall © 2004 Creative Teaching Press

Sentence/Story Builder

Directions: Use the pictures to help you write a sentence or story that describes who, what, when, where, and why.

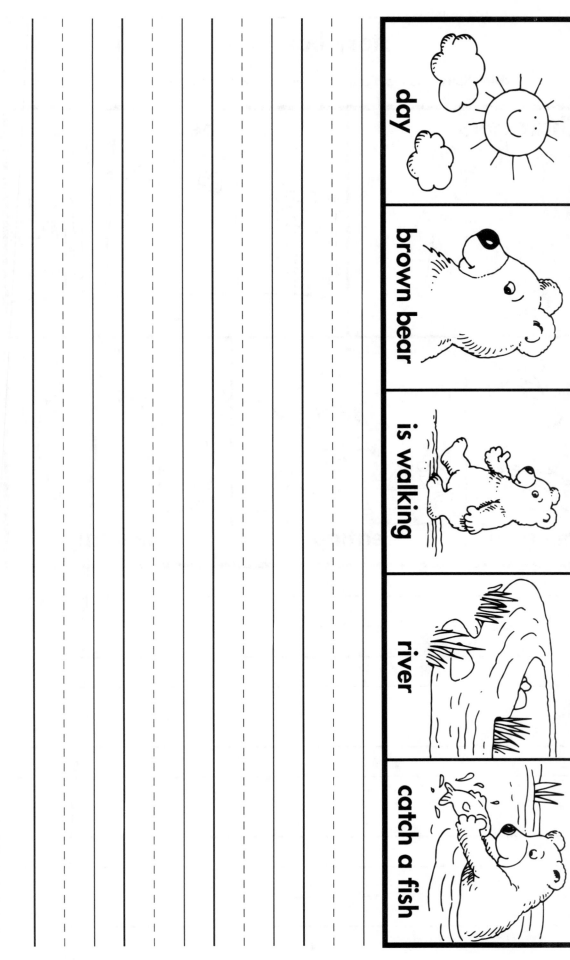

When	Who	Is Doing What	Where	Why
day	brown bear	is walking	river	catch a fish

Name_____

Story Box

Directions: Use the picture box ideas to write a story.

Characters

bears

Setting

ZOO

zoo

1 swimming

2 eating

3 sleeping

_____
- -
_____
- -
_____
- -
_____
- -
_____

Rebus Writing • Fall © 2004 Creative Teaching Press

Backward Story

Directions: Read the ending of the story and then tell what might have happened at the beginning and in the middle of the story.

QUESTIONS FOR PROMPTING
• What did the bear look like?
• What kind of bear was it?
• Where did it live?
• Why did the bear go into the cave?
• What did it have to do first?
• What did it do while it was in the cave? What do we call that?

n+🔨   😛+●   ☝   人   w+🏃   ✚   ☀+"E"   👉   🐻

Now   that   it   was   warm   and   sunny,   the   bear

"K"+m   ↗   of   👉   ⛰   2   look   4   f+👻+d

came   out   of   the   cave   to   look   for   food.

Let's Create It

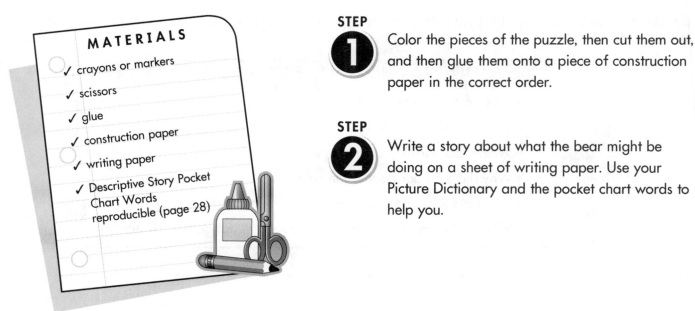

MATERIALS

✓ crayons or markers

✓ scissors

✓ glue

✓ construction paper

✓ writing paper

✓ Descriptive Story Pocket Chart Words reproducible (page 28)

STEP 1
Color the pieces of the puzzle, then cut them out, and then glue them onto a piece of construction paper in the correct order.

STEP 2
Write a story about what the bear might be doing on a sheet of writing paper. Use your Picture Dictionary and the pocket chart words to help you.

A Bear Puzzle

Rebus Writing • Fall © 2004 Creative Teaching Press

Shape Book

Directions: Color your cover. Cut out the cover and writing paper to create a shape book.

Word Web

Directions: Use the words on the word web to help you write a story.

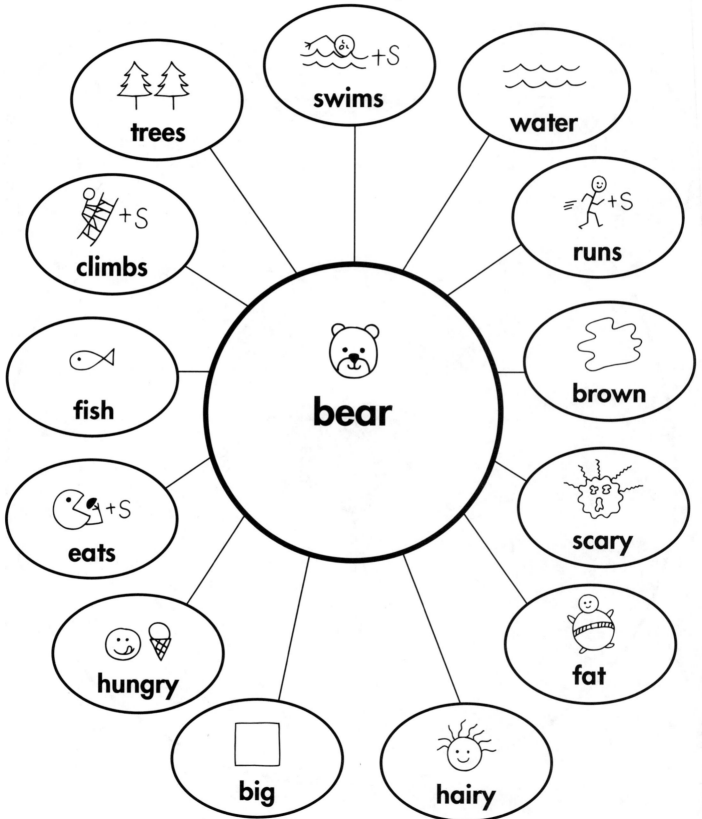

Rebus Writing • Fall © 2004 Creative Teaching Press

Class Book

Directions: Use words from your Picture Dictionary and around the room to help you complete the sentences. Draw a picture to go with your sentences.

_____ Bear,

_____ Bear,

What do you _____?

I _____ a _____

_____ at me!

By _____

Sequence Story

Directions: Color the pictures and cut them out. Glue the picture cards in order in the numbered boxes to show the sequence of the bear's hibernation. Use the picture cards to write a story on another piece of paper. Use your Picture Dictionary and the Sequence Story Pocket Chart Words to help you.

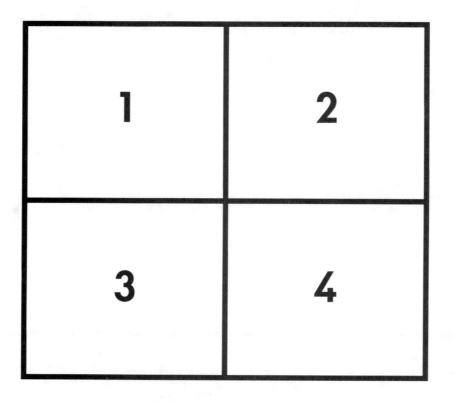

Pumpkins +S

Use this theme to teach the sequence of the growth cycle from seed to flower to pumpkin. The activities in this theme emphasize the use of describing words and sequence of events. Additional vocabulary is introduced to promote descriptive and seasonal writing related to harvest and Halloween.

READ-ALOUDS

The Pumpkin Book
by Gail Gibbons
(HOLIDAY HOUSE)

Pumpkin Circle: The Story of a Garden
by George Levenson
(TRICYCLE PRESS)

The Pumpkin Patch
by Elizabeth King
(PUFFIN)

Pumpkin Pumpkin
by Jeanne Titherington
(HARPERTROPHY)

Too Many Pumpkins
by Linda White
(HOLIDAY HOUSE)

PICTURE DICTIONARY WORDS

pumpkin
seed
plant
flower
grew
orange
giant
round
fat
big
little
pretty

POCKET CHART WORDS

Descriptive Story	Sequence Story
funny	vine
pretty	sprout
ugly	leaves
huge	pick
cute	carve
green	jack-o'-lantern

EMPHASIZE THESE HAVE-TO WORDS IN THIS THEME:

"R"
are
(when a letter is in quotes, it says its name)

▪
in
(the dot is in the box)

2
to

▪+2
into

saw
(a picture of a saw)

SENTENCE SQUARES SENTENCES

I see the orange pumpkin.
It is big and fat.
Look at the giant round pumpkin.
See the little pumpkin seeds.
The pumpkin is funny and scary.

SEQUENCE STORY PROMPT

Explain the life cycle of a pumpkin.

Picture Dictionary Words

Directions: Read each word. Cut out the picture cards and glue them in your Picture Dictionary.

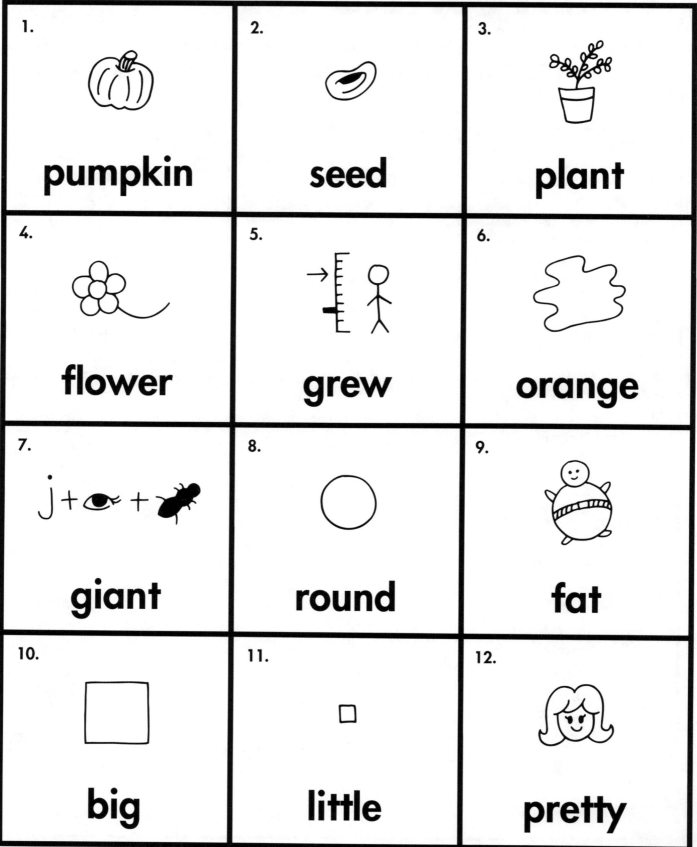

1. pumpkin

2. seed

3. plant

4. flower

5. grew

6. orange

7. giant

8. round

9. fat

10. big

11. little

12. pretty

Rebus Writing • Fall © 2004 Creative Teaching Press

Pocket Chart Words

Descriptive Story (Use with Let's Create It on page 55)

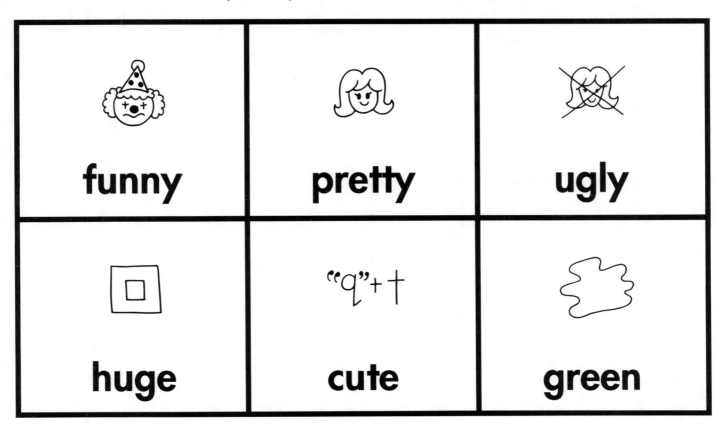

funny	pretty	ugly
huge	cute	green

Sequence Story (Use with Sequence Story on page 59)

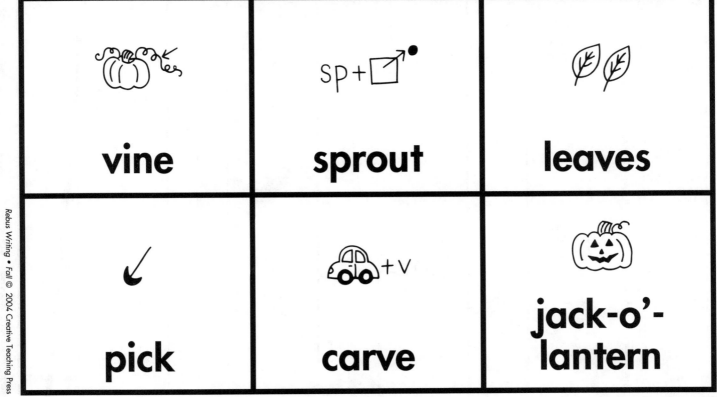

vine	sprout	leaves
pick	carve	jack-o'-lantern

Rebus Writing • Fall © 2004 Creative Teaching Press

Word Hunt

Directions: Use your Picture Dictionary to help you find the word that goes with each picture. Write the correct word below each picture. Complete the special sentence at the bottom of the page.

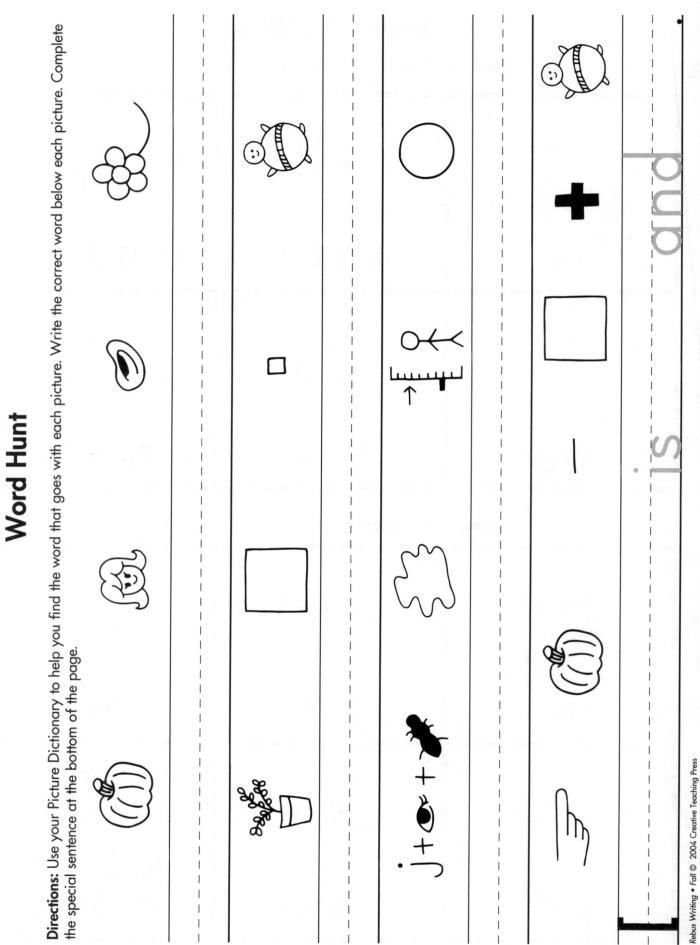

Secret Sentence Booklet

Directions: Write the correct word under each rebus picture.

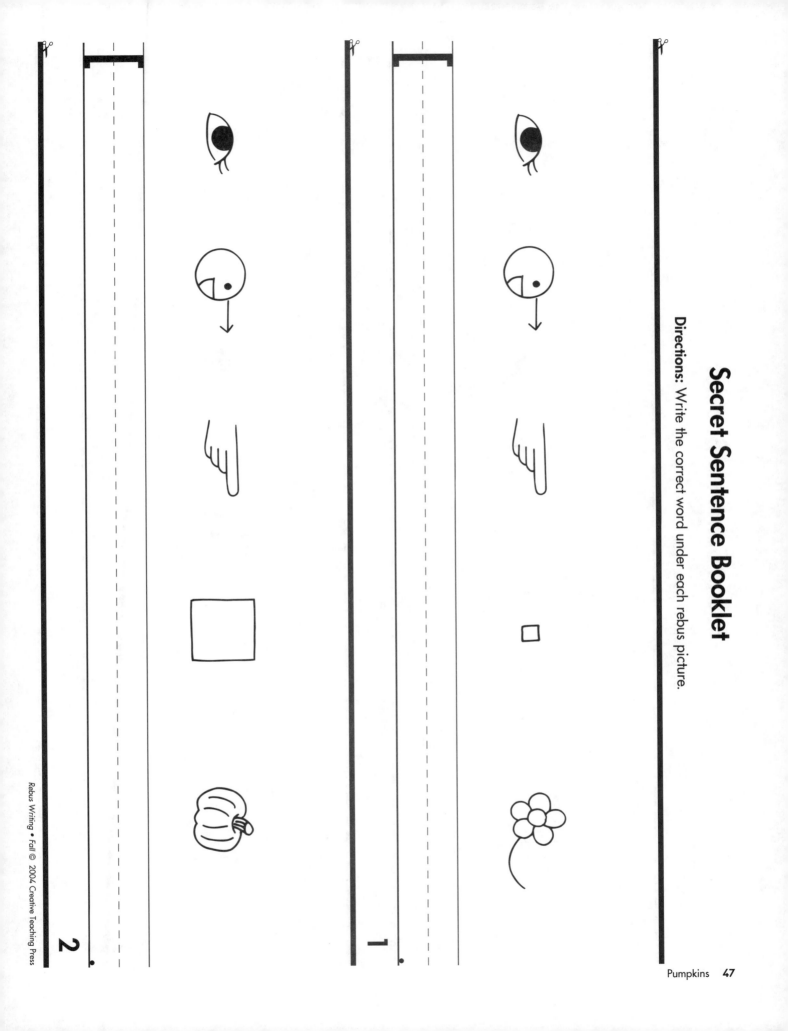

1

2

Secret Sentence Booklet

Directions: Write the correct word under each rebus picture.

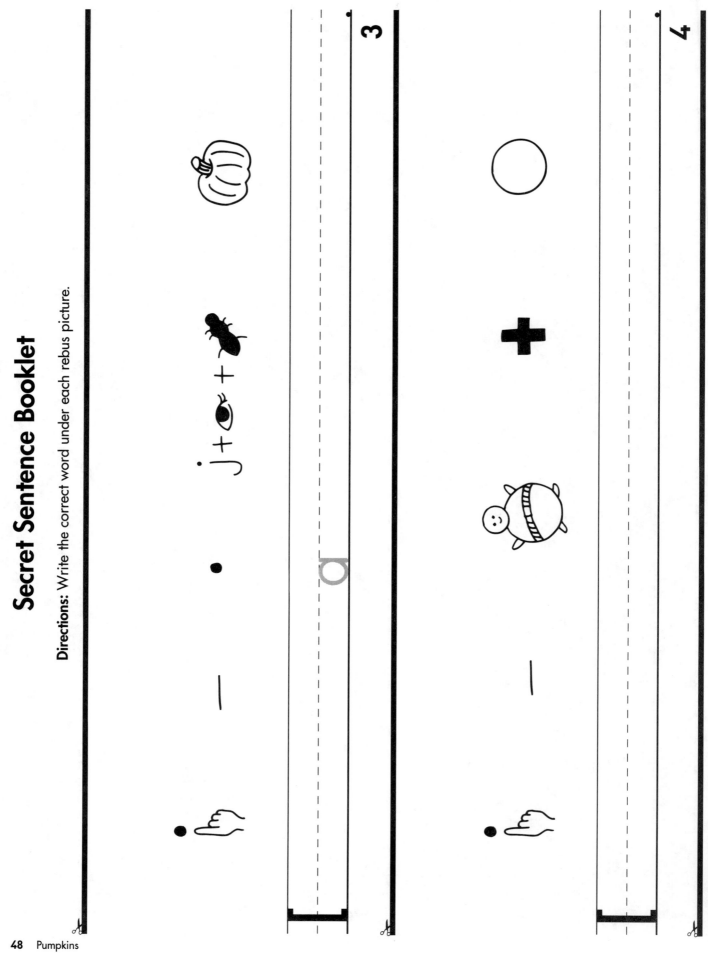

3

4

Rebus Writing • Fall © 2004 Creative Teaching Press

Name_____

Bubble Writing

Directions: Write the correct word in each bubble. Use these words to complete the sentences at the bottom of the page.

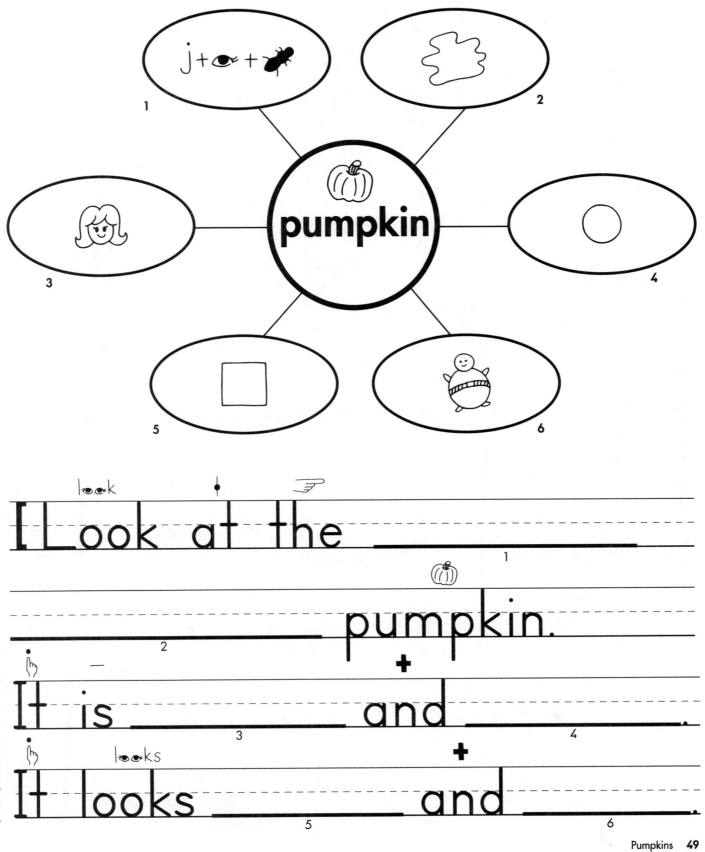

Connect a Sentence

Directions: Read the phrase in the center bubble. Add words from the connecting bubbles to the phrase to make a sentence. Use additional words to create more sentences. Write the sentences on a separate piece of paper.

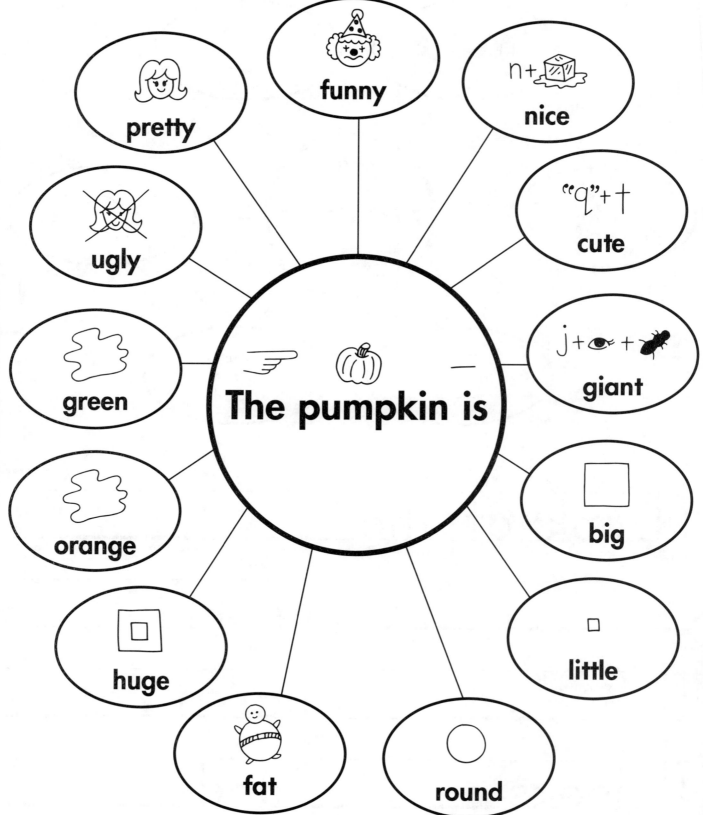

Rebus Writing • Fall © 2004 Creative Teaching Press

Sentence Squares

Directions: Read the word cards. Cut apart the cards and mix them up. Make sure that the words are face up. Use the word cards to make sentences.

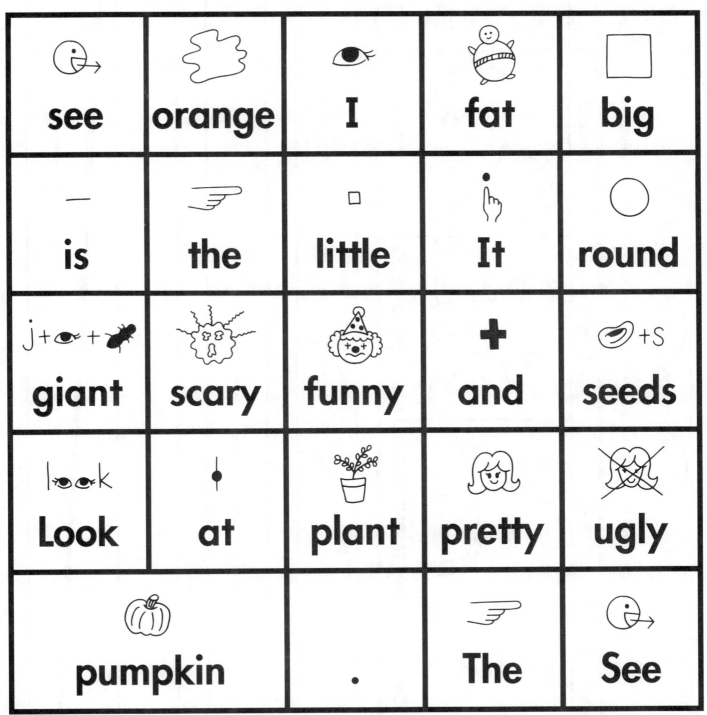

see	orange	I	fat	big
is	the	little	It	round
giant	scary	funny	and	seeds
Look	at	plant	pretty	ugly
pumpkin	.	The	See

Sentence/Story Builder

Directions: Use the pictures to help you write a sentence or story that describes **who, what, when, where, and why.**

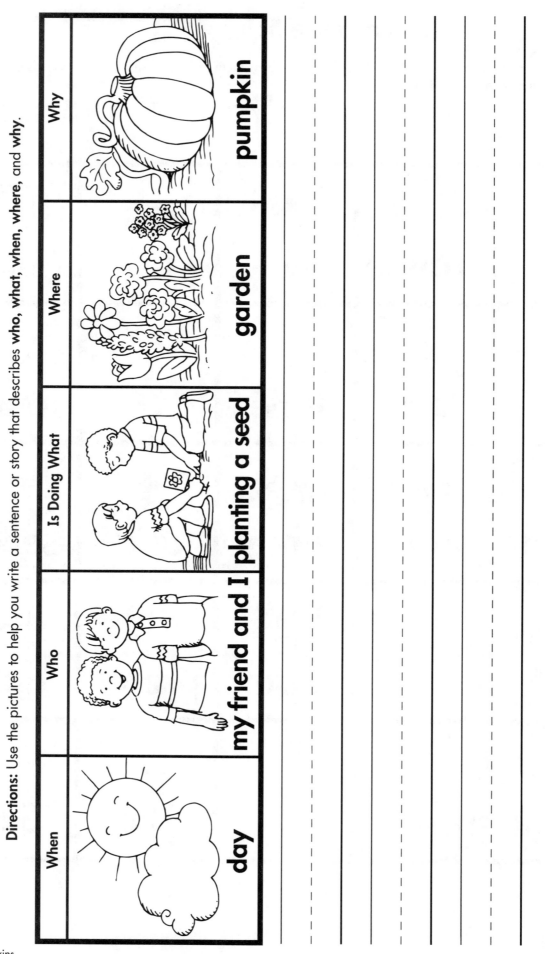

When	Who	Is Doing What	Where	Why
day	my friend and I	planting a seed	garden	pumpkin

Name_____

Story Box

Directions: Use the picture box ideas to write a story.

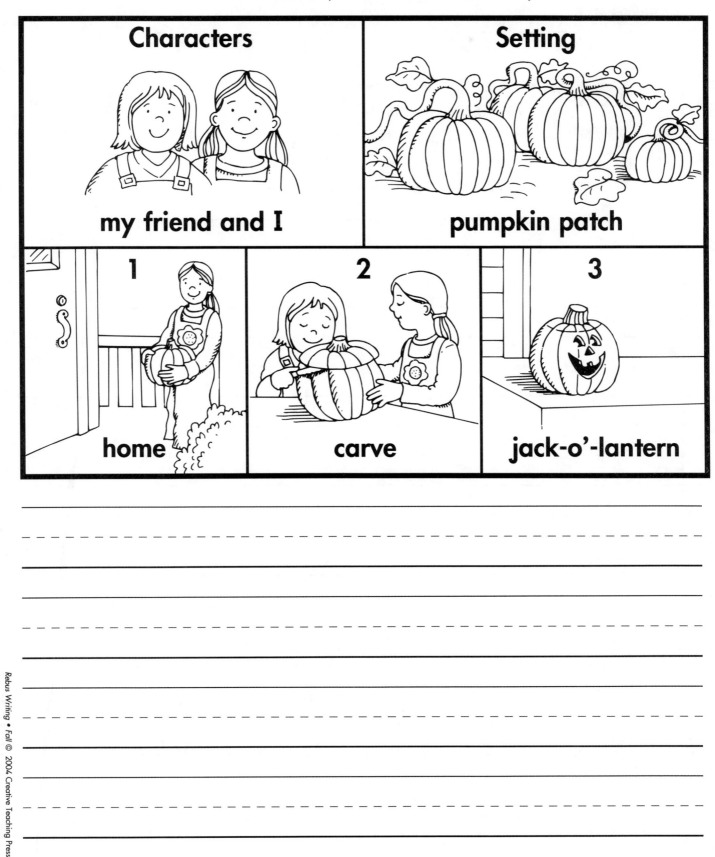

Characters

my friend and I

Setting

pumpkin patch

1 home

2 carve

3 jack-o'-lantern

_____
- - - - - - - - - - - - - - - - - -
_____
- - - - - - - - - - - - - - - - - -
_____
- - - - - - - - - - - - - - - - - -
_____
- - - - - - - - - - - - - - - - - -
_____
- - - - - - - - - - - - - - - - - -

Rebus Writing • Fall © 2004 Creative Teaching Press

Backward Story

Directions: Read the ending of the story and then tell what might have happened at the beginning and in the middle of the story.

QUESTIONS FOR PROMPTING

- How did the pumpkin start out?
- What did you do with the seed?
- Why did you plant it?
- What happened after you planted the seed?
- What did you have to do to make it grow?

Now   it   is   a   big,   giant,   orange   pumpkin.

Rebus Writing • Fall © 2004 Creative Teaching Press

Let's Create It

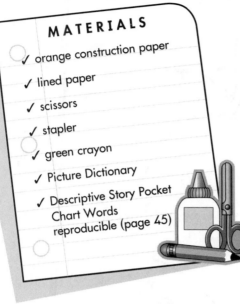

MATERIALS

✓ orange construction paper

✓ lined paper

✓ scissors

✓ stapler

✓ green crayon

✓ Picture Dictionary

✓ Descriptive Story Pocket Chart Words reproducible (page 45)

(Note to the teacher: Copy a class set of the pumpkin pattern on orange construction paper. Cut a piece of lined paper into the shape of a pumpkin for each child.)

STEP 1 Cut out both halves of the pumpkin pattern. Place the lined paper underneath the pumpkin halves. Staple the paper together on the designated lines. Use a green crayon to color the pumpkin stem.

STEP 2 Write a story about the pumpkin on the lined paper. Use your Picture Dictionary and the pocket chart words to help you.

Peek-a-Boo Pumpkin

Shape Book

Directions: Color your cover. Cut out the cover and writing paper to create a shape book.

Word Web

Directions: Use the words on the word web to help you write a story.

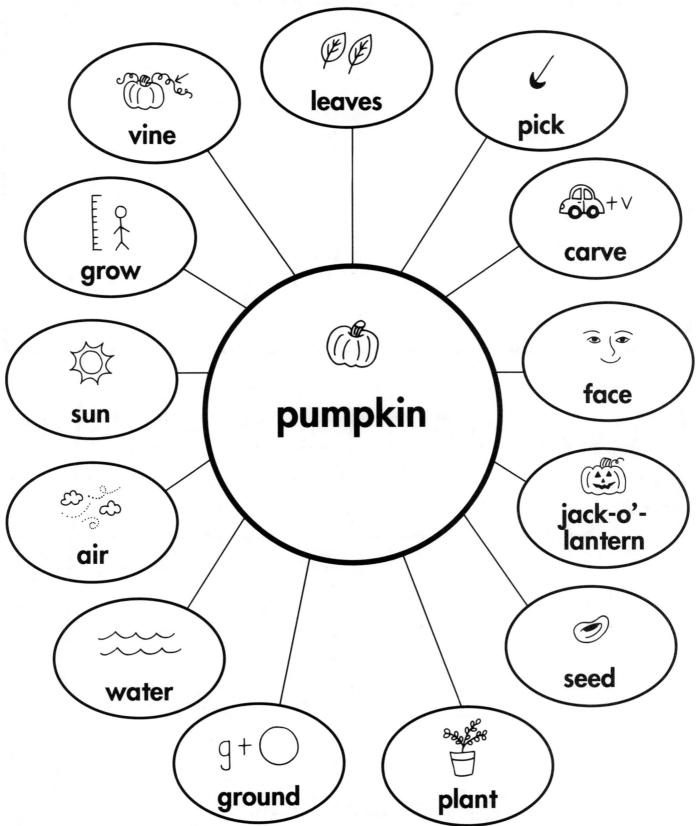

Class Book

Directions: Use words from your Picture Dictionary and around the room to help you complete the sentences. Draw a picture to go with your sentences.

Look at the pumpkin.

It is _____,

_____, and

_____.

By _____

Rebus Writing • Fall © 2004 Creative Teaching Press

Sequence Story

Directions: Color the pictures and cut them out. Glue the picture cards in order in the numbered boxes to show the growth of a pumpkin. Use the picture cards to write a story on another piece of paper. Use your Picture Dictionary and the Sequence Story Pocket Chart Words to help you.

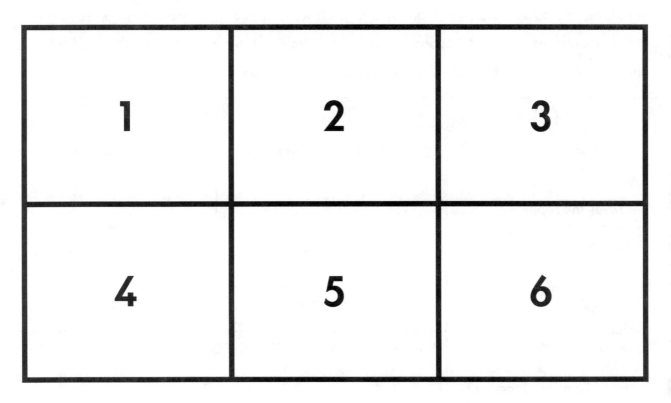

Bats

b● + s

Use this theme to teach information about bats using rebuses. The activities in this theme emphasize the use of describing words, naming words, and doing words, which are used to teach word functions. The word endings -er, -ing, and -y are also introduced. Additional vocabulary is introduced to expand the knowledge of bats and to promote descriptive and seasonal writing related to Halloween.

READ-ALOUDS

Bat Jamboree
by Kathi Appelt
(HARPERTROPHY)

Bat Loves the Night
by Nicola Davies
(CANDLEWICK PRESS)

Bats
by Gail Gibbons
(HOLIDAY HOUSE)

Stellaluna
by Janell Cannon
(HARCOURT)

Zipping, Zapping, Zooming Bats
by Ann Earle
(SCOTT FORESMAN)

PICTURE DICTIONARY WORDS

bat
gray
furry
tiny
wings
ears
fly
hang
hunt
eat
insects
cave

POCKET CHART WORDS

Descriptive Story	Sequence Story
wide wings	night
hairy body	dark
tiny ears	sleep
sharp teeth	upside down
round eyes	trees
sharp claws	day

EMPHASIZE THESE HAVE-TO WORDS IN THIS THEME:

was

have
(I have the dot)

had
(I had the dot, but I dropped it)

like
(I like you)

has
(/h/ + /s/)

SENTENCE SQUARES SENTENCES

I saw the scary bat.
The bat likes to eat insects.
The tiny bat hangs in a cave.
Look at the furry bat.
I saw the bat fly into the cave.

SEQUENCE STORY PROMPT

Explain what a typical day for a bat is like.

Picture Dictionary Words

Directions: Read each word. Cut out the picture cards and glue them in your Picture Dictionary.

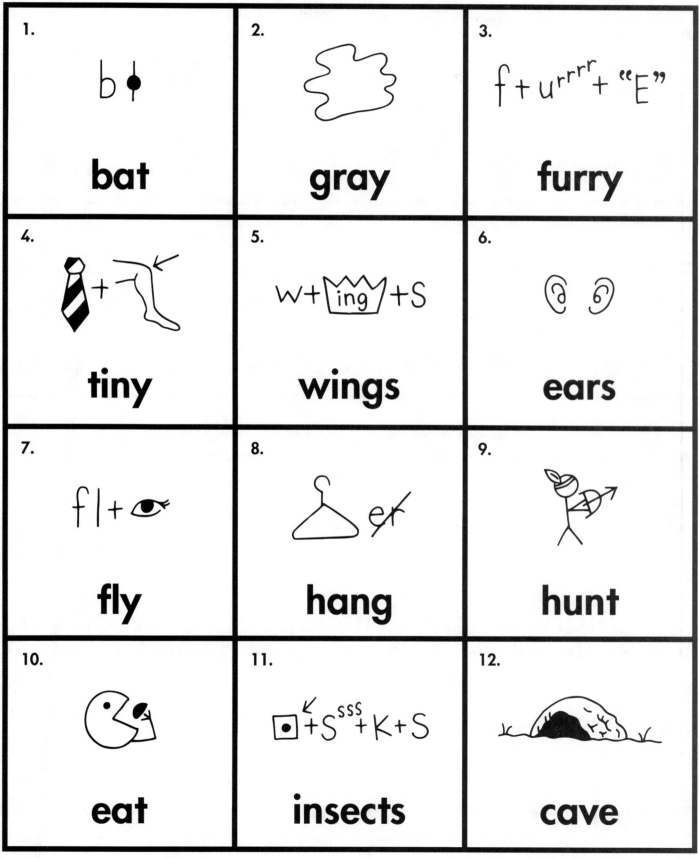

1. bat

2. gray

3. furry

4. tiny

5. wings

6. ears

7. fly

8. hang

9. hunt

10. eat

11. insects

12. cave

Pocket Chart Words

Descriptive Story (Use with Let's Create It on page 72)

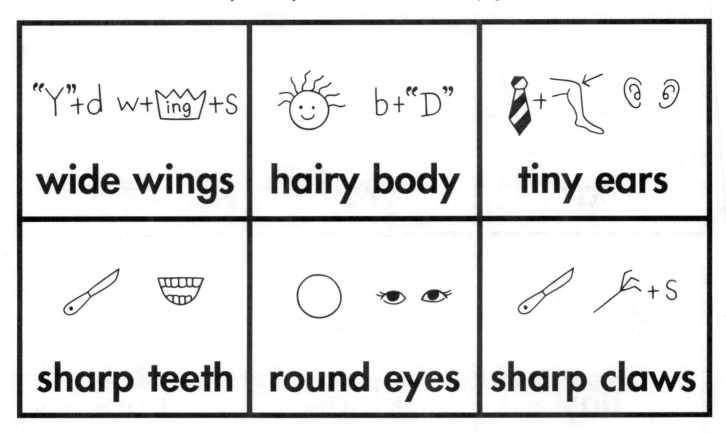

"Y"+d w+[ing]+S	b+"D"	
wide wings	**hairy body**	**tiny ears**
		+S
sharp teeth	**round eyes**	**sharp claws**

Sequence Story (Use with Sequence Story on page 76)

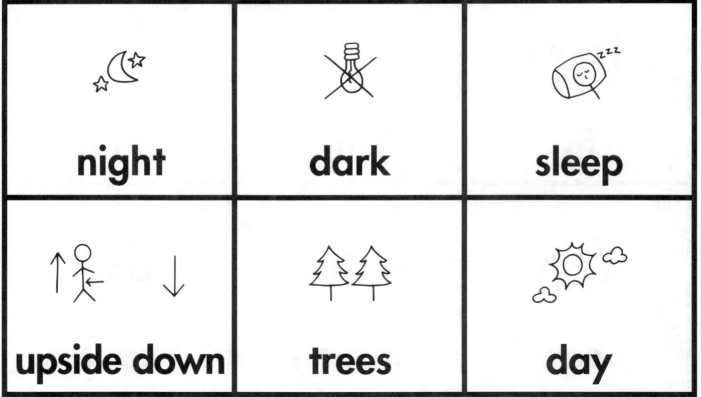

night	**dark**	**sleep**
upside down	**trees**	**day**

Rebus Writing • Fall © 2004 Creative Teaching Press

Name _____

Word Hunt

Directions: Use your Picture Dictionary to help you find the word that goes with each picture. Write the correct word below each picture. Complete the special sentence at the bottom of the page.

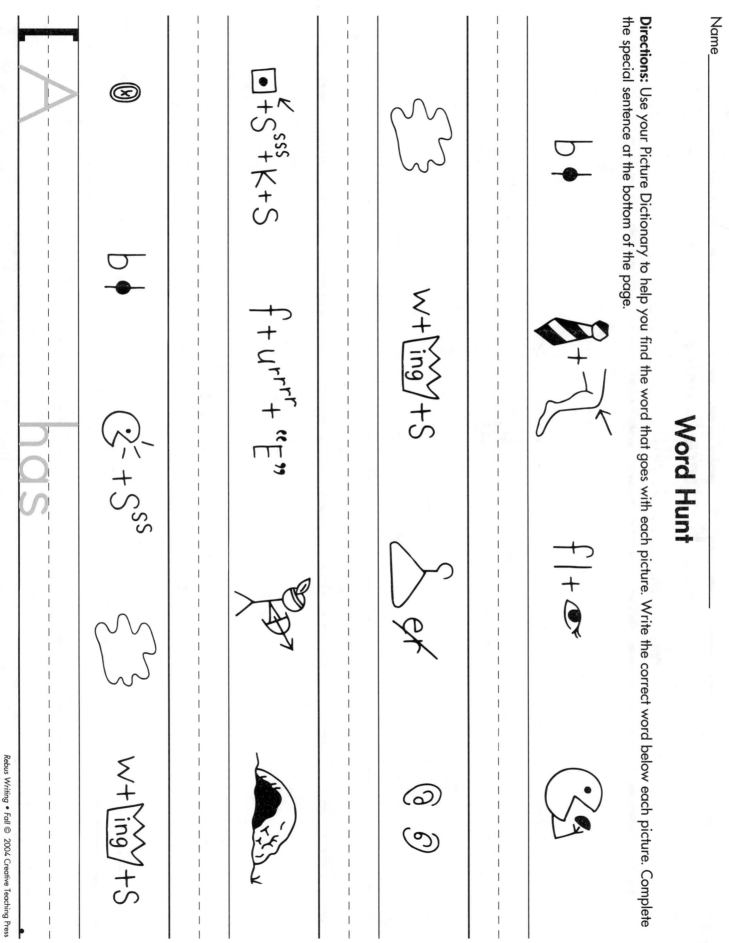

Secret Sentence Booklet

Directions: Write the correct word under each rebus picture.

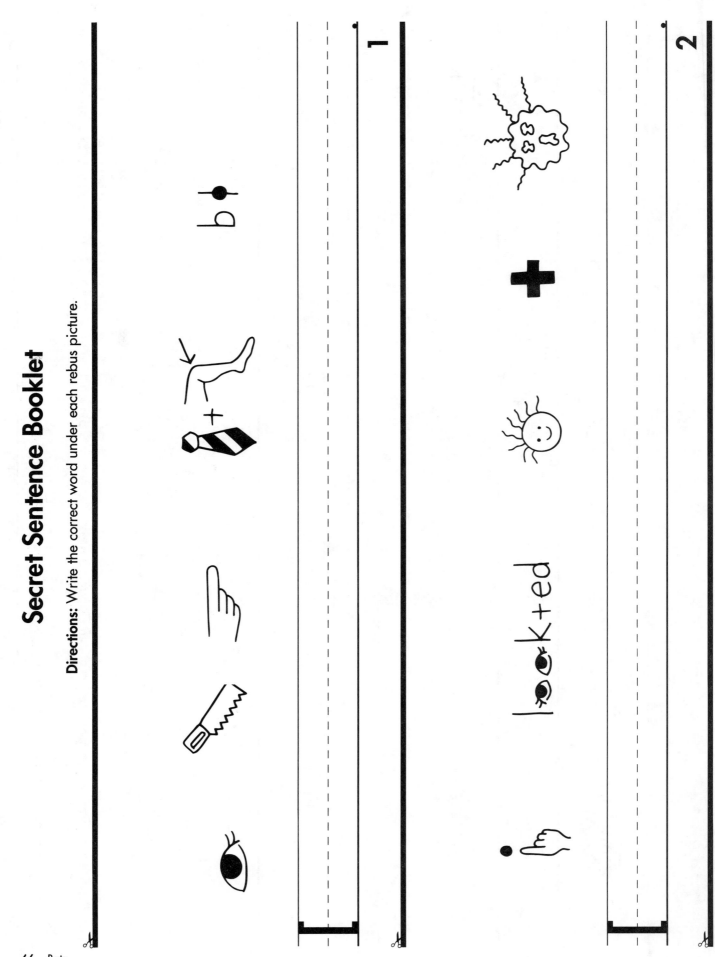

1

2

Secret Sentence Booklet

Directions: Write the correct word under each rebus picture.

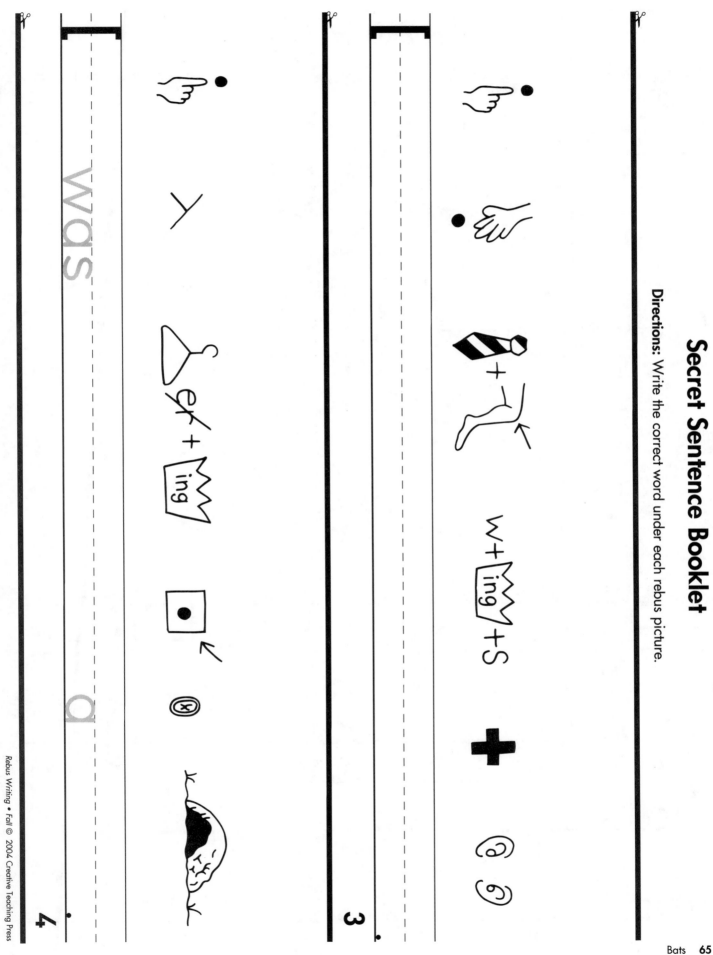

Bubble Writing

Directions: Write the correct word in each bubble. Use these words to complete the sentences at the bottom of the page.

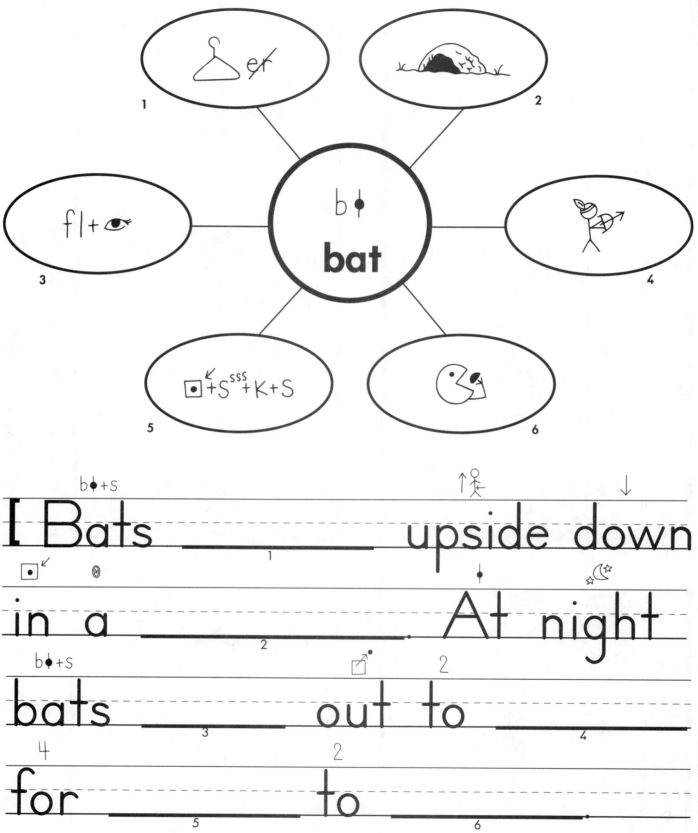

Rebus Writing • Fall © 2004 Creative Teaching Press

Connect a Sentence

Directions: Read the phrase in the center bubble. Add words from the connecting bubbles to the phrase to make a sentence. Use additional words to create more sentences. Write the sentences on a separate piece of paper.

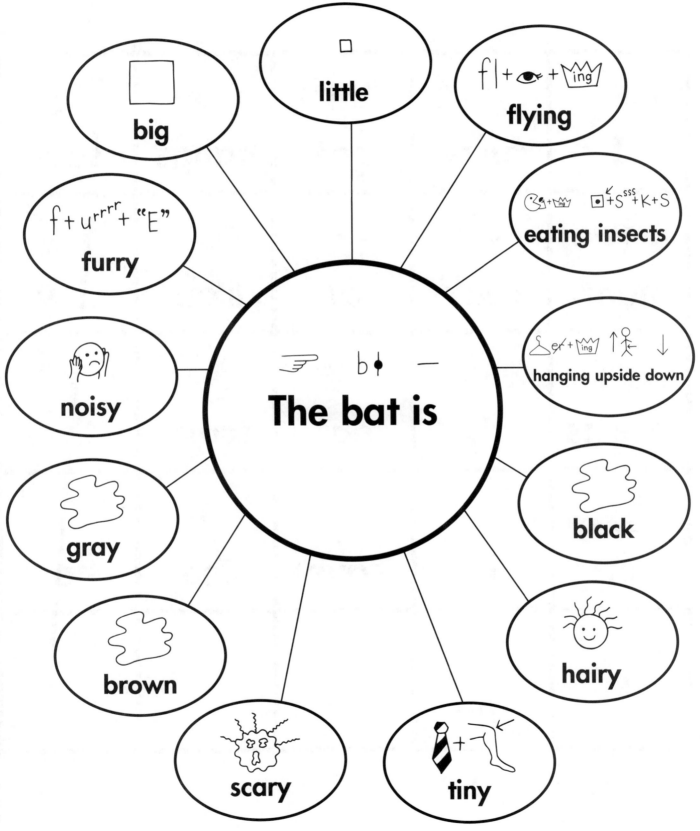

Sentence Squares

Directions: Read the word cards. Cut apart the cards and mix them up. Make sure that the words are face up. Use the word cards to make sentences.

I	furry	bat	hangs	saw
hunt	Look	at	likes	tiny
insects	fly	eat	scary	the
in	is	cave	the	to
.	The			

Rebus Writing • Fall © 2004 Creative Teaching Press

Sentence/Story Builder

Directions: Use the pictures to help you write a sentence or story that describes who, what, when, where, and why.

When	Who	Is Doing What	Where	Why
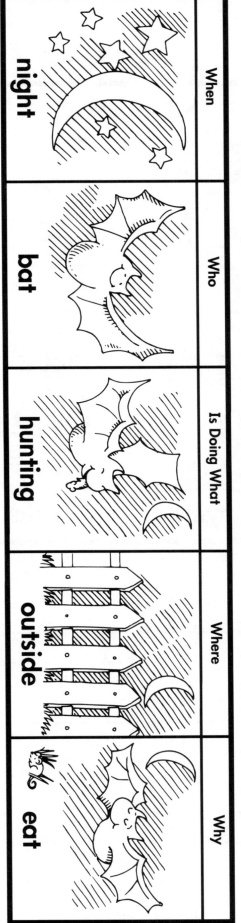 night	bat	hunting	outside	eat

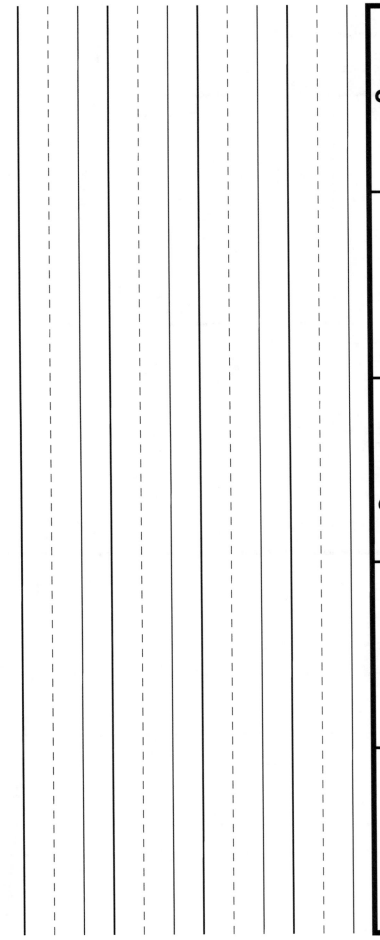

Story Box

Directions: Use the picture box ideas to write a story.

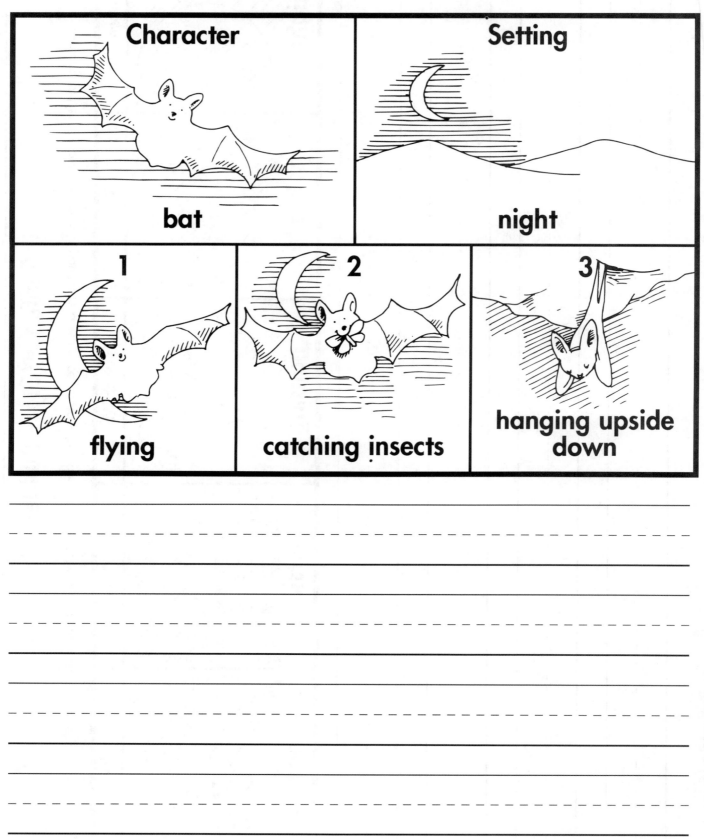

Character

bat

Setting

night

1 flying

2 catching insects

3 hanging upside down

_____

- -

_____

- -

_____

- -

_____

- -

_____

Rebus Writing • Fall © 2004 Creative Teaching Press

Backward Story

Directions: Read the ending of the story and then tell what might have happened at the beginning and in the middle of the story.

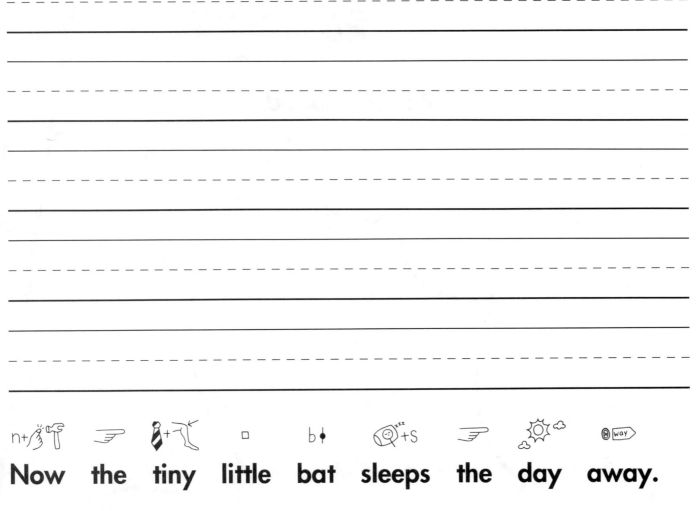

QUESTIONS FOR PROMPTING

- Why is the bat tired?
- Why is the bat sleeping during the day?
- What did the bat do during the night?

Now the tiny little bat sleeps the day away.

Let's Create It

(Note to the teacher: Copy a class set of the bat pattern on heavy tagboard or card stock.)

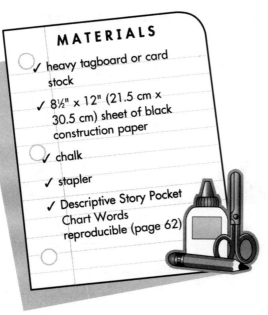

MATERIALS

✓ heavy tagboard or card stock

✓ 8½" x 12" (21.5 cm x 30.5 cm) sheet of black construction paper

✓ chalk

✓ stapler

✓ Descriptive Story Pocket Chart Words reproducible (page 62)

STEP 1

Fold a sheet of black construction paper in half. Place the straight edge of the bat pattern on the fold. Use chalk to trace the pattern onto the paper. Cut out the bat and use the chalk to add features to it. Use the leftover section of the construction paper to make a wristband by cutting out a rectangular strip. Staple the bat in the middle of the strip. Size the black strip to your wrist and cut off the excess paper. Staple the wristband.

STEP 2

Write a story describing how the bat looks. Use your Picture Dictionary and the pocket chart words to help you.

Bat Wristband

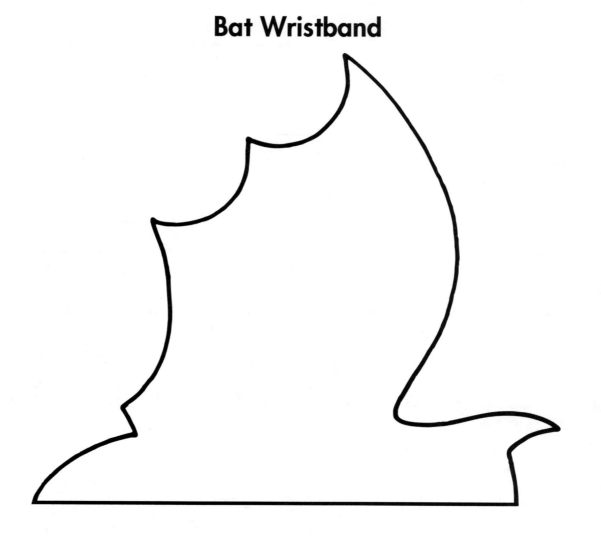

Rebus Writing • Fall © 2004 Creative Teaching Press

Shape Book

Directions: Color your cover. Cut out the cover and writing paper to create a shape book.

Word Web

Directions: Use the words on the word web to help you write a story.

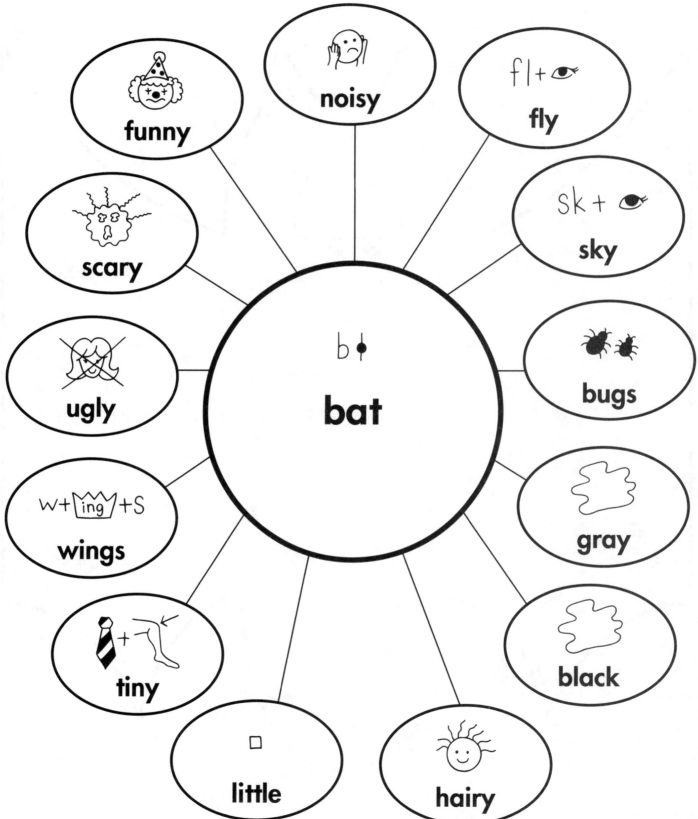

Class Book

Directions: Use words from your Picture Dictionary and around the room to help you complete the sentences. Draw a picture to go with your sentences.

Scary bat, scary bat, what can you do? I can

By _____

Sequence Story

Directions: Color the pictures and cut them out. Glue the picture cards in order in the numbered boxes to show the sequence of the bat's day. Use the picture cards to write a story on another piece of paper. Use your Picture Dictionary and the Sequence Story Pocket Chart Words to help you.

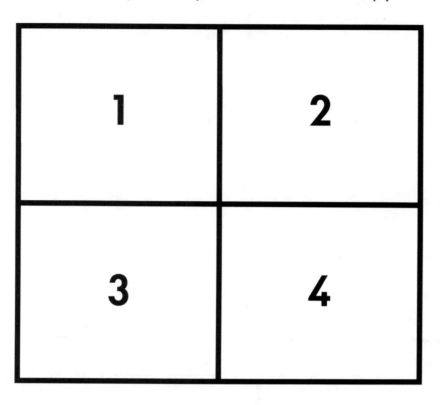

Spiders

+S

The activities in this theme emphasize the use of describing words and sequence of events. Additional vocabulary is introduced to promote descriptive and informational writing related to spiders.

READ-ALOUDS

Be Nice to Spiders
by Margaret Bloy Graham
(HARPERCOLLINS)

Sophie's Masterpiece: A Spider's Tale
by Eileen Spinelli
(SIMON & SCHUSTER)

Spiders
by Gail Gibbons
(HOLIDAY HOUSE)

Spiders Spin Webs
by Yvonne Winer
(CHARLESBRIDGE PUBLISHING)

The Very Busy Spider
by Eric Carle
(PHILOMEL BOOKS)

PICTURE DICTIONARY WORDS

spider
red
spin
web
legs
eight
hairy
eggs
lay
eyes
fangs
jump

POCKET CHART WORDS

Descriptive Story	Sequence Story
round eyes	spinnerets
hairy body	silk
spots	stick
claws	catch
sharp fangs	prey
strong jaws	poison

EMPHASIZE THESE HAVE-TO WORDS IN THIS THEME:

m+"A"+K	S+ⓐ+m			☺+"A"
make	**some**	**can**	**not**	**they**
			(to tie a knot)	(stick out your tongue and say "A")

SENTENCE SQUARES SENTENCES

I saw the big spider.
The spider has eight eyes.
Look at the big ugly fangs.
The hairy spider lays eggs.
The spider has eight hairy legs.
Look at the spider spin a web.

SEQUENCE STORY PROMPT

Explain how a spider spins its web.

Picture Dictionary Words

Directions: Read each word. Cut out the picture cards and glue them in your Picture Dictionary.

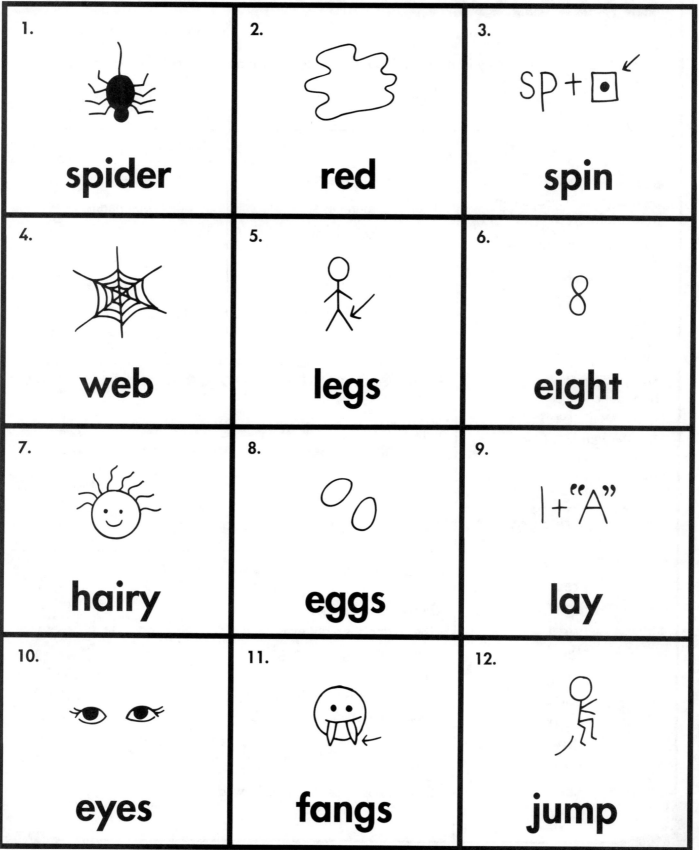

1. spider	2. red	3. spin
4. web	5. legs	6. eight
7. hairy	8. eggs	9. lay
10. eyes	11. fangs	12. jump

Pocket Chart Words

Descriptive Story (Use with Let's Create It on page 89)

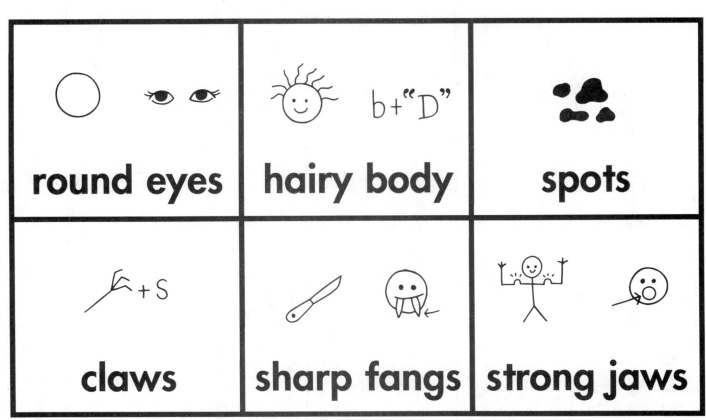

round eyes	hairy body	spots
claws	sharp fangs	strong jaws

Sequence Story (Use with Sequence Story on page 93)

spinnerets	silk	stick
catch	prey	poison

Name _____

Word Hunt

Directions: Use your Picture Dictionary to help you find the word that goes with each picture. Write the correct word below each picture. Complete the special sentence at the bottom of the page.

Rebus Writing • Fall © 2004 Creative Teaching Press

Secret Sentence Booklet

Directions: Write the correct word under each rebus picture.

S+ⓧ+m 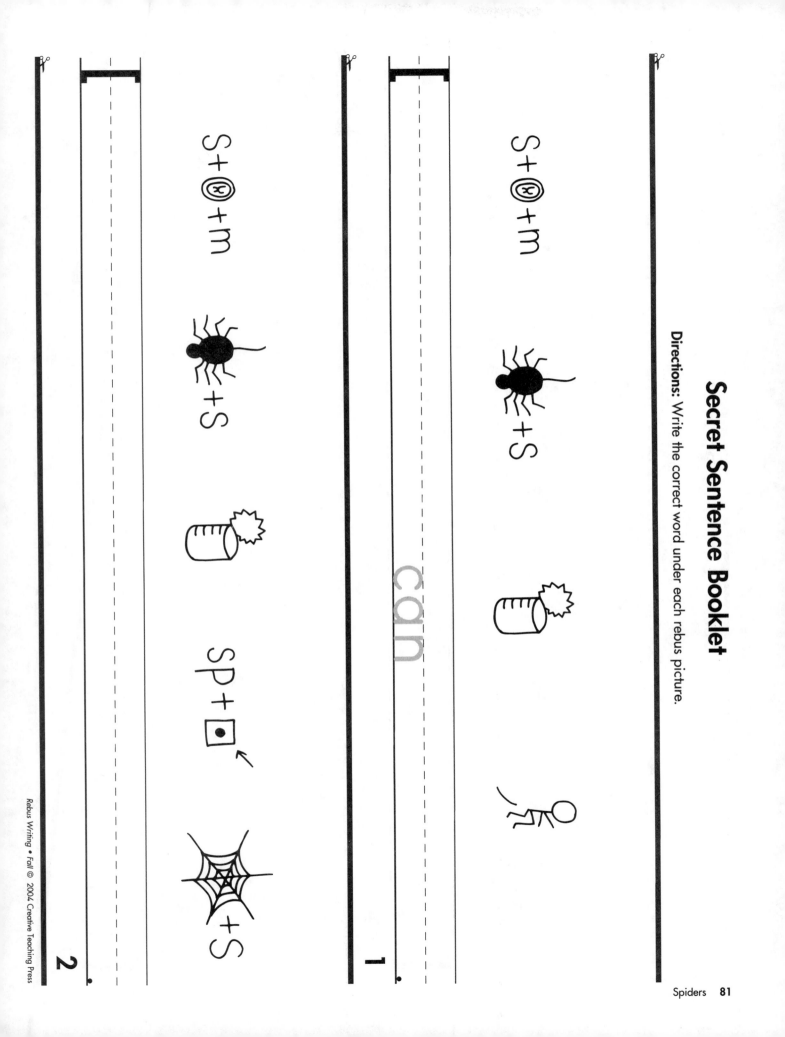 +S 🗲 ⤾

can

S+ⓧ+m +S 🗲 SP+▫↖ +S

Secret Sentence Booklet

Directions: Write the correct word under each rebus picture.

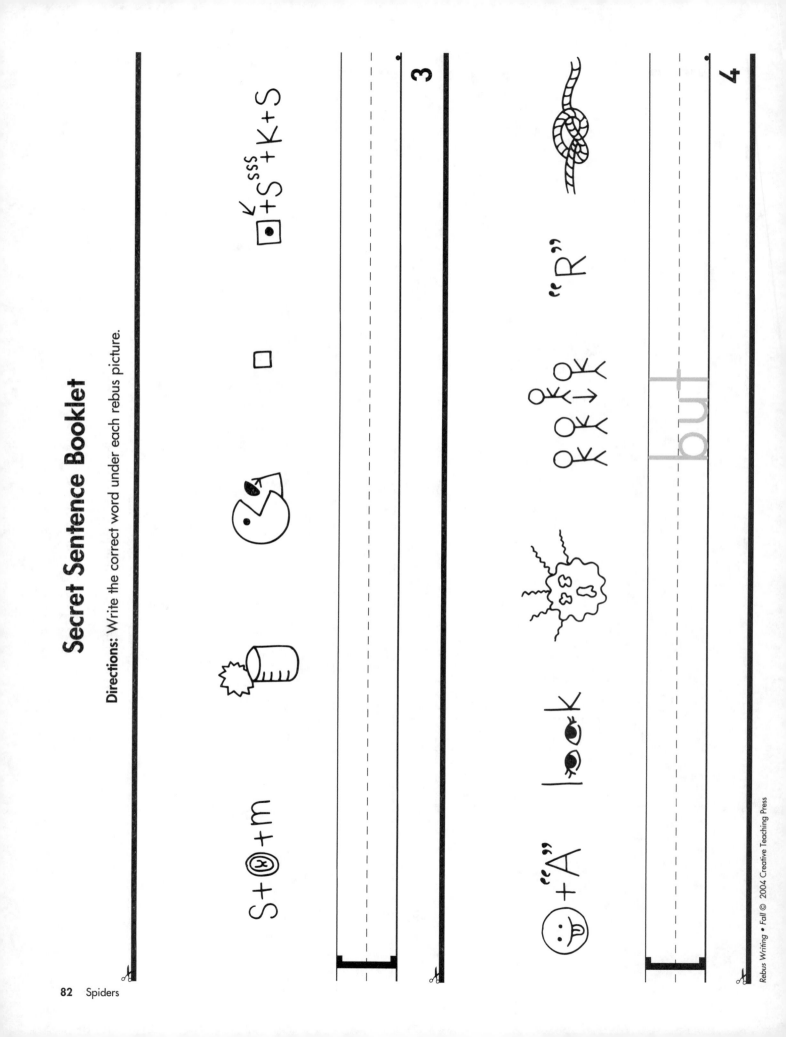

3

4

Name_____

Bubble Writing

Directions: Write the correct word in each bubble. Use these words to complete the sentences at the bottom of the page.

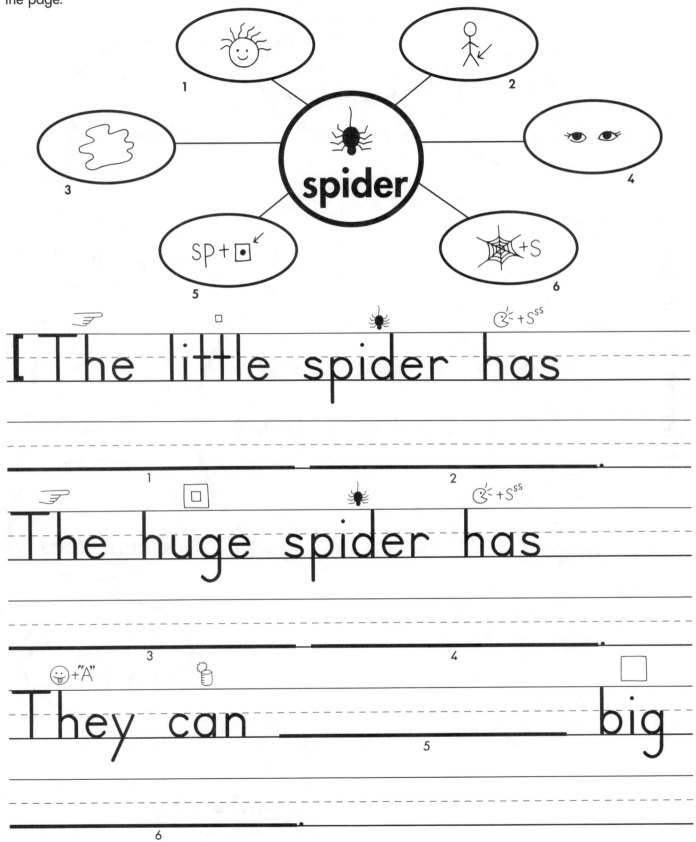

Connect a Sentence

Directions: Read the phrase in the center bubble. Add words from the connecting bubbles to the phrase to make a sentence. Use additional words to create more sentences. Write the sentences on a separate piece of paper.

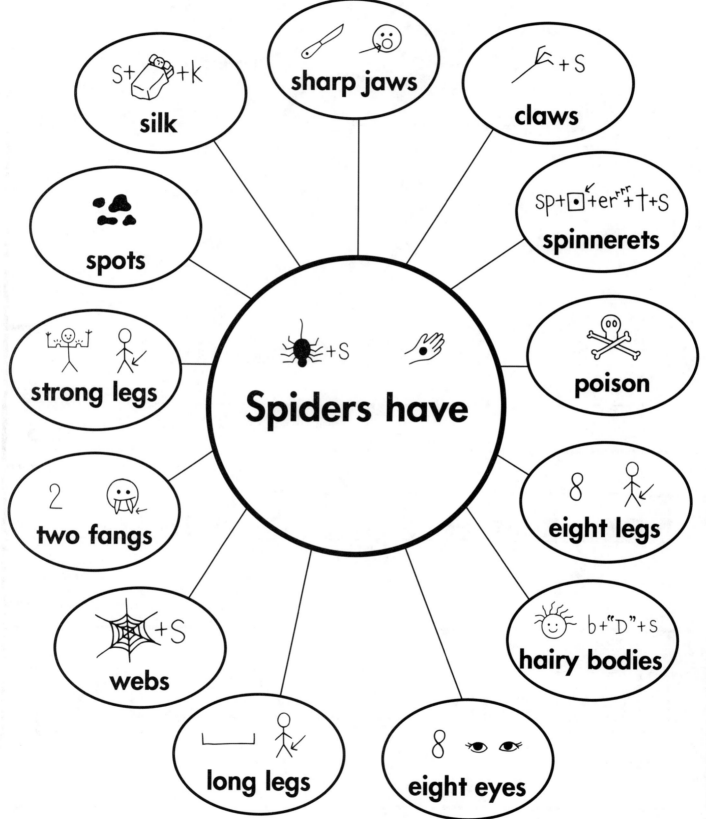

Rebus Writing • Fall © 2004 Creative Teaching Press

Sentence Squares

Directions: Read the word cards. Cut apart the cards and mix them up. Make sure that the words are face up. Use the word cards to make sentences.

I	web	spider	spin	saw
Look	big	at	eight	eyes
a	the	lays	hairy	fangs
has	eggs	ugly	is	legs
.	The			

Sentence/Story Builder

Directions: Use the pictures to help you write a sentence or story that describes **who, what, when, where,** and **why.**

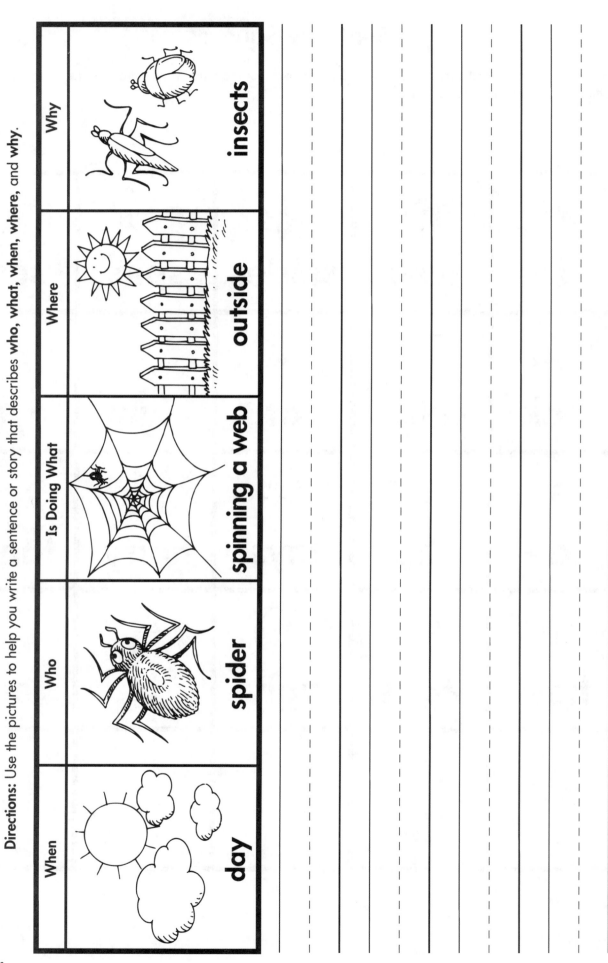

When	Who	Is Doing What	Where	Why
day	spider	spinning a web	outside	insects

Rebus Writing • Fall © 2004 Creative Teaching Press

Name_____

Story Box

Directions: Use the picture box ideas to write a story.

Character

Little Miss Muffet

Setting

garden

1 walking

2 sitting

3 running

_____
- - - - - - - - - - - - - - - - - - -
_____
- - - - - - - - - - - - - - - - - - -
_____
- - - - - - - - - - - - - - - - - - -
_____
- - - - - - - - - - - - - - - - - - -
_____
- - - - - - - - - - - - - - - - - - -
_____

Name_____

Backward Story

Directions: Read the ending of the story and then tell what might have happened at the beginning and in the middle of the story.

QUESTIONS FOR PROMPTING
• What did the spider look like?
• Why was it near the water spout?
• What happened when it rained?
• Why did the spider go up the water spout?

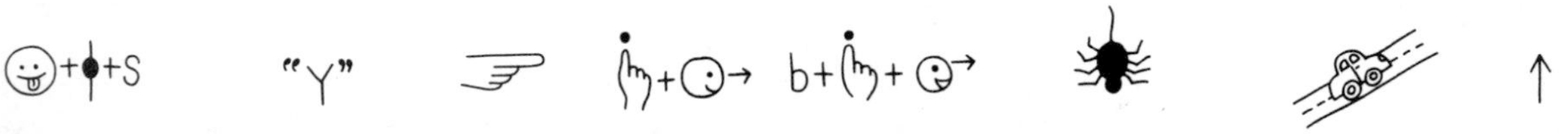

_____

_____

_____

_____

_____

_____

_____

_____

_____

_____

That's   why   the   Itsy   Bitsy   Spider   went   up

the   water   spout.

Rebus Writing • Fall © 2004 Creative Teaching Press

Let's Create It

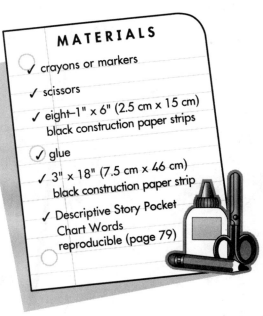

MATERIALS

✓ crayons or markers

✓ scissors

✓ eight–1" x 6" (2.5 cm x 15 cm) black construction paper strips

✓ glue

✓ 3" x 18" (7.5 cm x 46 cm) black construction paper strip

✓ Descriptive Story Pocket Chart Words reproducible (page 79)

STEP

Draw a spider's face on the circle and then cut it out. Fold the eight small strips accordion style. Glue the spider's face to the center of the large construction paper strip. Glue four small strips to each side of the large strip. Have your teacher staple the band to fit around your head.

STEP

Write a story about your spider on a separate piece of paper. Use your Picture Dictionary and the pocket chart words to help you.

Spider Headband

Rebus Writing • Fall © 2004 Creative Teaching Press

Shape Book

Directions: Color your cover. Cut out the cover and writing paper to create a shape book.

Rebus Writing • Fall © 2004 Creative Teaching Press

Word Web

Directions: Use the words on the word web to help you write a story.

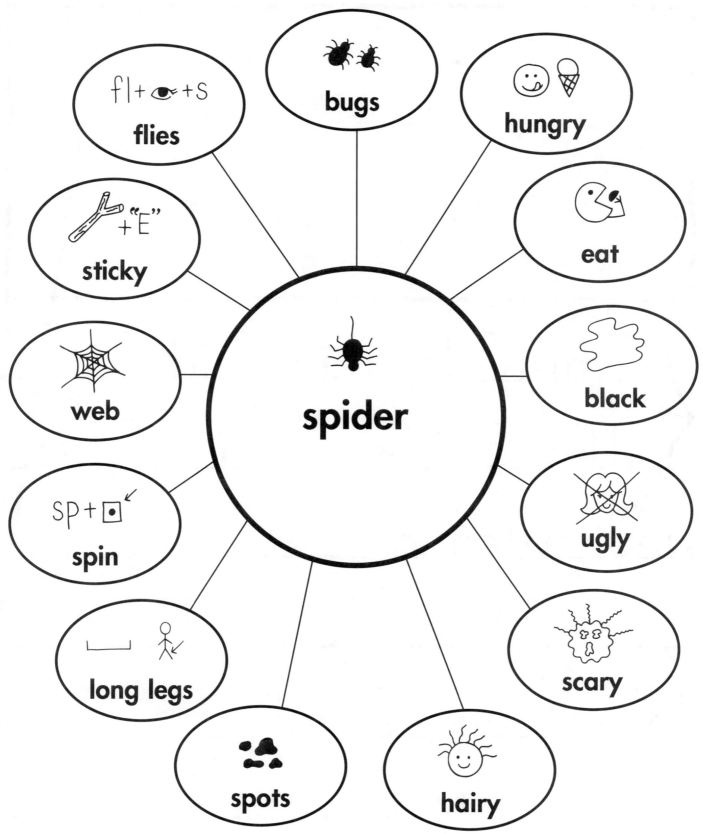

Rebus Writing • Fall © 2004 Creative Teaching Press

Class Book

Directions: Use words from your Picture Dictionary and around the room to help you complete the sentences. Draw a picture to go with your sentences.

Mommy Spider said,

"Little Spider, spin a web,

and catch a _____

_____

_____

to eat on bread!"

By _____

Rebus Writing • Fall © 2004 Creative Teaching Press

Sequence Story

Directions: Color the pictures and cut them out. Glue the picture cards in order in the numbered boxes to show the sequence of the spider spinning the web. Use the picture cards to write a story on another piece of paper. Use your Picture Dictionary and the Sequence Story Pocket Chart Words to help you.

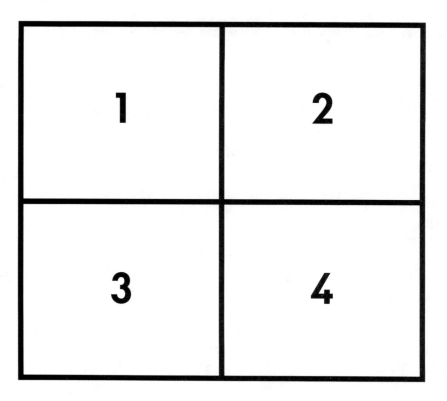

Indians

 +s

The activities in this theme emphasize the use of describing words and sequence of events. Additional vocabulary is introduced to promote descriptive and seasonal writing related to Thanksgiving.

READ-ALOUDS

Giving Thanks: A Native American Good Morning Message by Jake Swamp
(LEE AND LOW BOOKS)

Knots on a Counting Rope by John Archambault and Bill Martin Jr.
(HENRY HOLT & COMPANY)

Nickommoh!: A Thanksgiving Celebration by Marcia Sewall
(ATHENEUM)

Squanto and the Miracle of Thanksgiving by Eric Metaxas
(THOMAS NELSON)

Squanto's Journey: The Story of the First Thanksgiving by Joseph Bruchac
(SILVER WHISTLE)

PICTURE DICTIONARY WORDS

Indian
boy
girl
brave
friendly
help
hunt
animals
food
fish
canoe
bow and arrow

POCKET CHART WORDS

Descriptive Story	Sequence Story
brown face	animal skins
animal feathers	clothes
headband	river
colorful paint	fire
brave (boy)	cook
squaw (girl)	clay

EMPHASIZE THESE HAVE-TO WORDS IN THIS THEME:

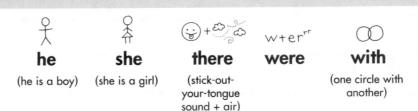

he
(he is a boy)

she
(she is a girl)

there
(stick-out-your-tongue sound + air)

were

with
(one circle with another)

SENTENCE SQUARES SENTENCES

The Indian was friendly.
The brave Indian liked to hunt.
Look at the brave little Indian.
The strong Indian boy was nice.
The Indian girl liked to help.

SEQUENCE STORY PROMPT

Explain how Indians lived long ago.

Picture Dictionary Words

Directions: Read each word. Cut out the picture cards and glue them in your Picture Dictionary.

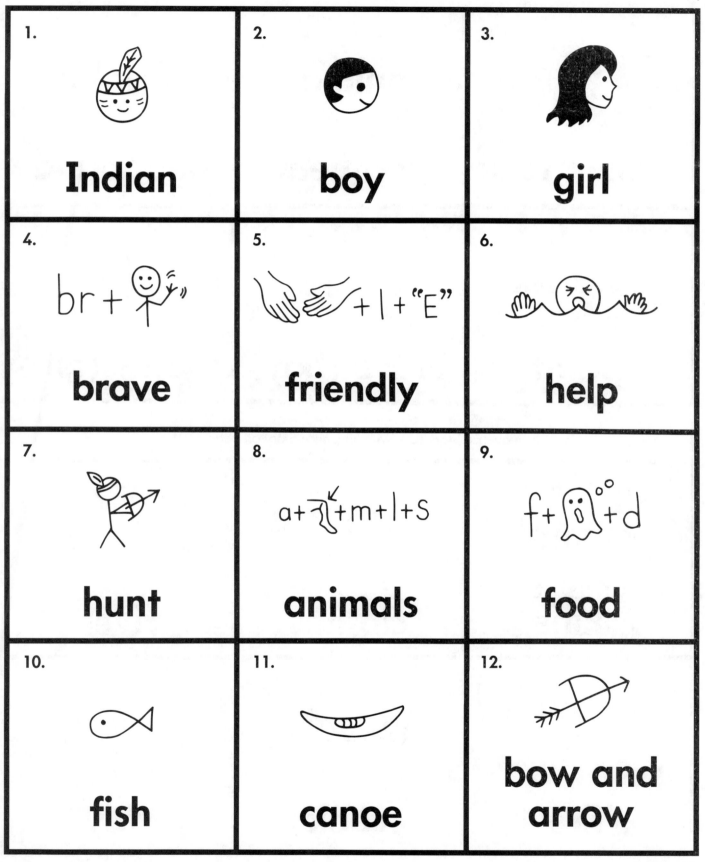

1. **Indian**	2. **boy**	3. **girl**
4. **brave**	5. **friendly**	6. **help**
7. **hunt**	8. **animals**	9. **food**
10. **fish**	11. **canoe**	12. **bow and arrow**

Pocket Chart Words

Descriptive Story (Use with Let's Create It on page 106)

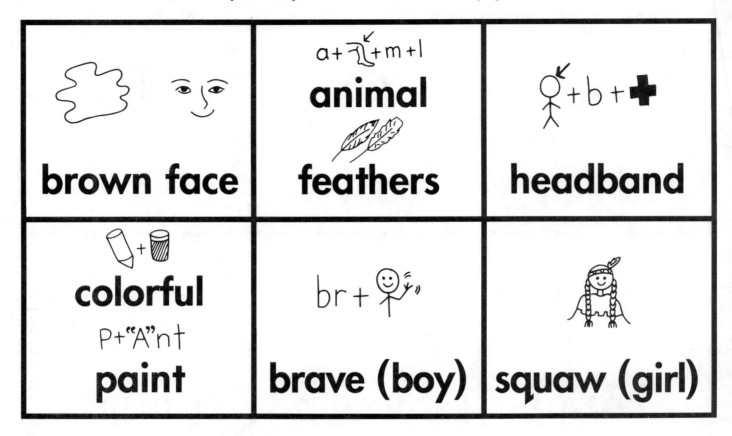

Sequence Story (Use with Sequence Story on page 110)

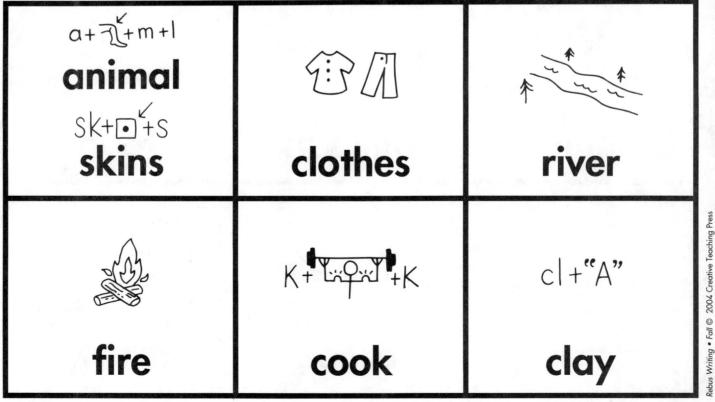

Rebus Writing • Fall © 2004 Creative Teaching Press

Name _____

Word Hunt

Directions: Use your Picture Dictionary to help you find the word that goes with each picture. Write the correct word below each picture. Complete the special sentence at the bottom of the page.

Rebus Writing • Fall © 2004 Creative Teaching Press

Secret Sentence Booklet

Directions: Write the correct word under each rebus picture.

1.

2.

had

Rebus Writing • Fall © 2004 Creative Teaching Press

Secret Sentence Booklet

Directions: Write the correct word under each rebus picture.

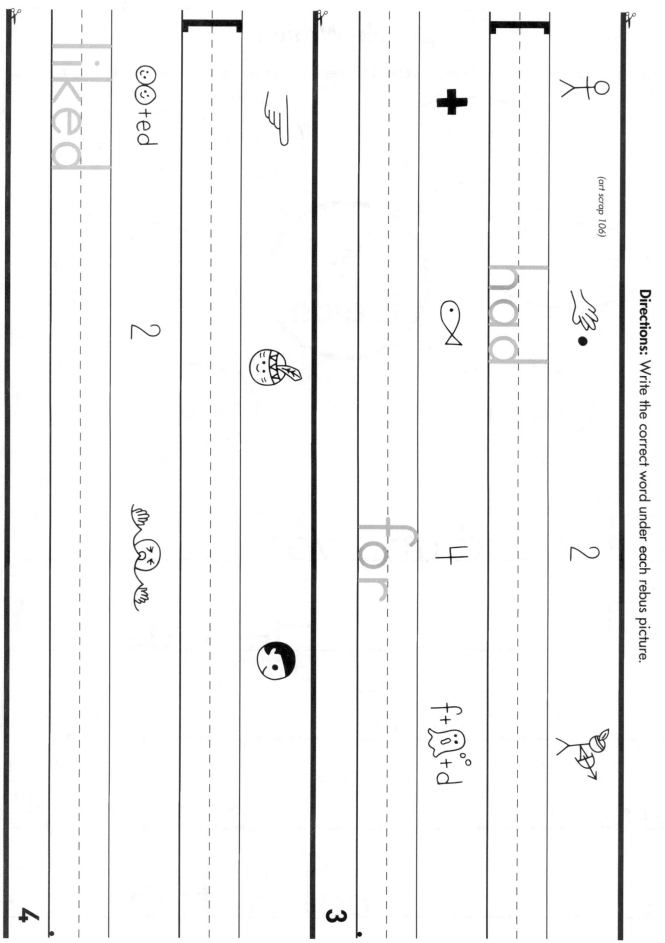

(art scrap 106)

1. had

2. +

3. for

4. liked

Bubble Writing

Directions: Write the correct word in each bubble. Use these words to complete the sentences at the bottom of the page.

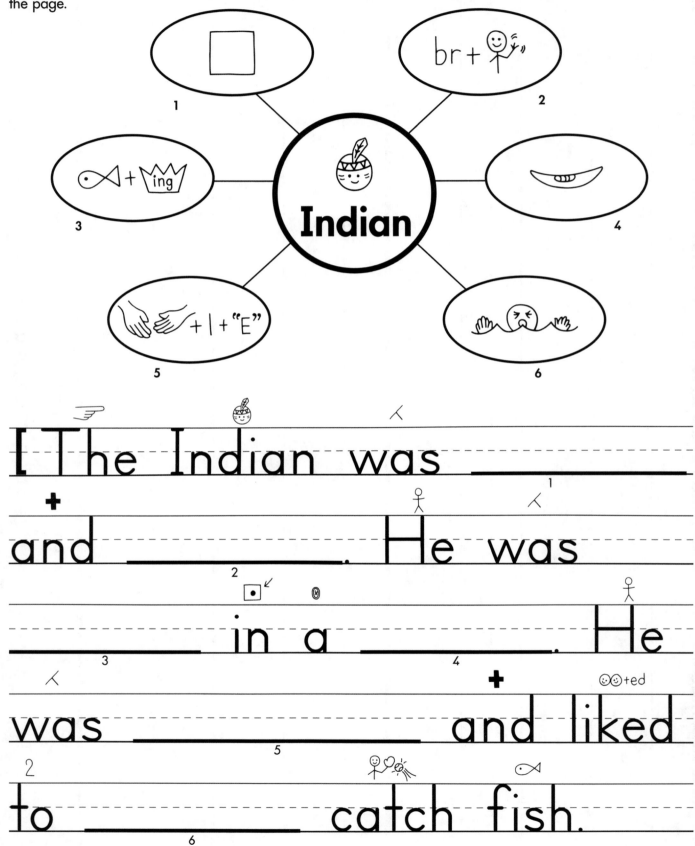

Connect a Sentence

Directions: Read the phrase in the center bubble. Add words from the connecting bubbles to the phrase to make a sentence. Use additional words to create more sentences. Write the sentences on a separate piece of paper.

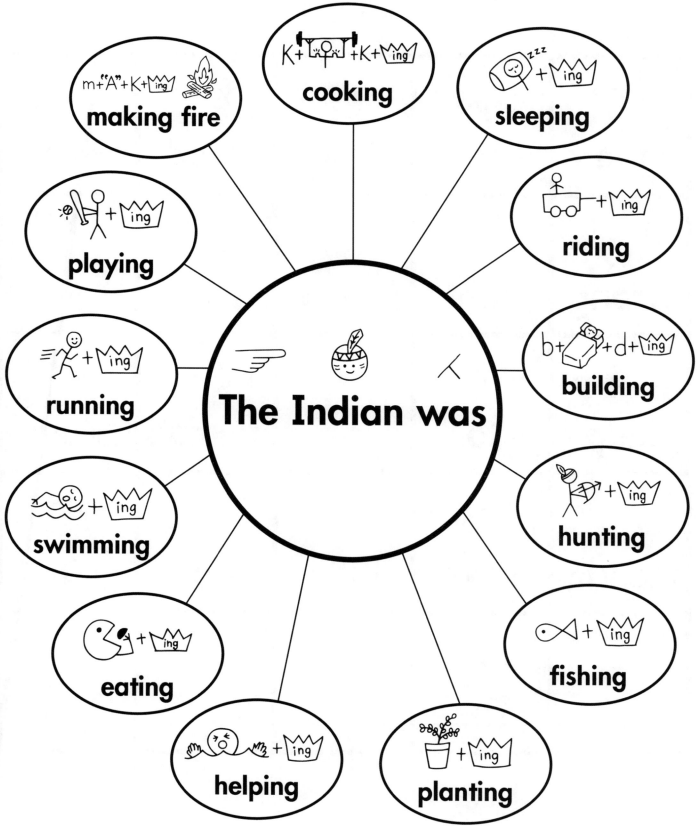

Sentence Squares

Directions: Read the word cards. Cut apart the cards and mix them up. Make sure that the words are face up. Use the word cards to make sentences.

the	**Look**	**boy**	liked	for
strong	hunt	**Indian**	was	girl
help	to	at	**animals**	brave
friendly	saw	little	food	nice
.	**The**			

Sentence/Story Builder

Directions: Use the pictures to help you write a sentence or story that describes **who, what, when, where,** and **why.**

When	Who	Is Doing What	Where	Why
 A long time ago	Indian	hunting	forest	food

_ _

_____

_ _

_____

_ _

_____

_ _

_____

Story Box

Directions: Use the picture box ideas to write a story.

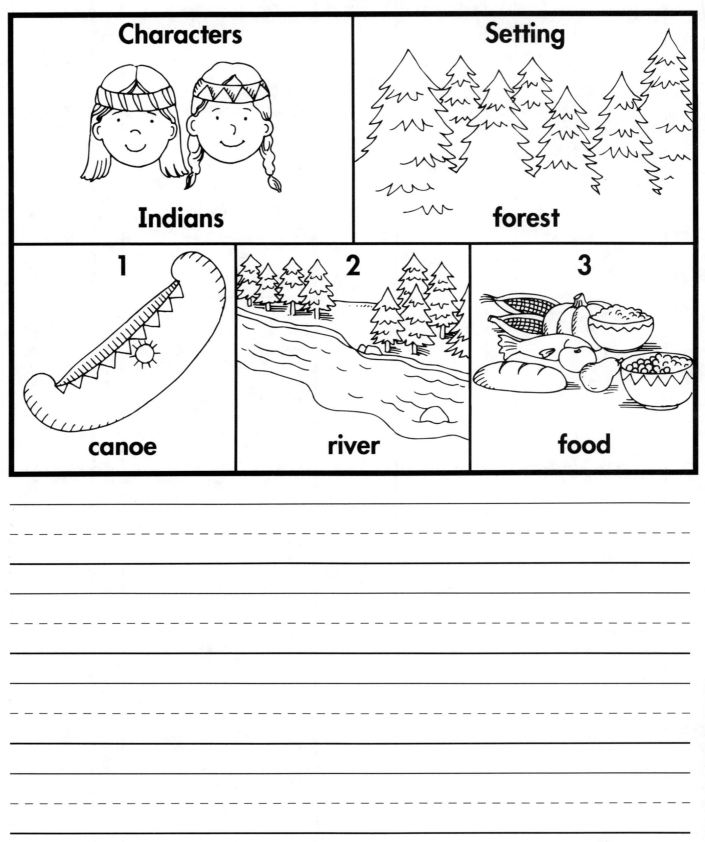

Characters

Indians

Setting

forest

1

canoe

2

river

3

food

Rebus Writing • Fall © 2004 Creative Teaching Press

Backward Story

Directions: Read the ending of the story and then tell what might have happened at the beginning and in the middle of the story.

```
QUESTIONS FOR PROMPTING

• What did the Indians have to do when they got up each morning?
• How did they get their food, clothing, blankets, dishes, etc.?
```

_____

- -

_____

- -

_____

- -

_____

- -

_____

- -

After   a   long   day,   the   Indians   went   to   sleep.

Let's Create It

MATERIALS

- ✓ brown construction paper or brown paper from a grocery bag
- ✓ scissors
- ✓ a hole punch
- ✓ yarn
- ✓ writing paper
- ✓ Descriptive Story Pocket Chart Words reproducible (page 96)

STEP 1 Fold a sheet of brown paper in half. Place the straight edge of the canoe pattern on the fold. Use a pencil to trace the pattern onto the paper. Cut out the canoe and keep the paper folded. Hole punch 6 holes along the left and right sides of your canoe. Weave a piece of yarn through the holes.

STEP 2 Write a story about an Indian on a separate sheet of writing paper. Use your Picture Dictionary and the pocket chart words to help you.

Canoe

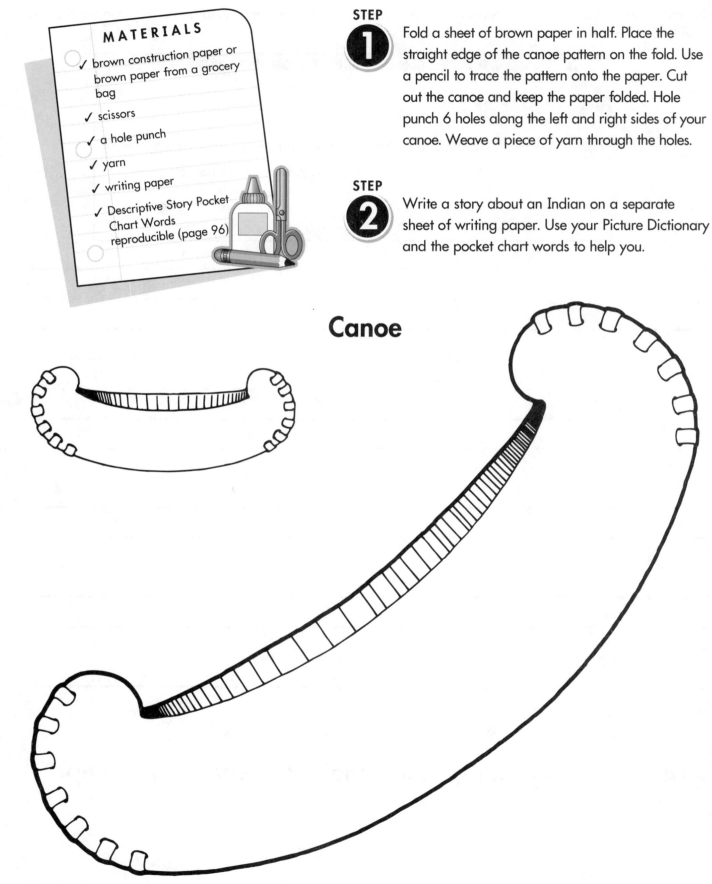

Shape Book

Directions: Color your cover. Cut out the cover and writing paper to create a shape book.

Word Web

Directions: Use the words on the word web to help you write a story.

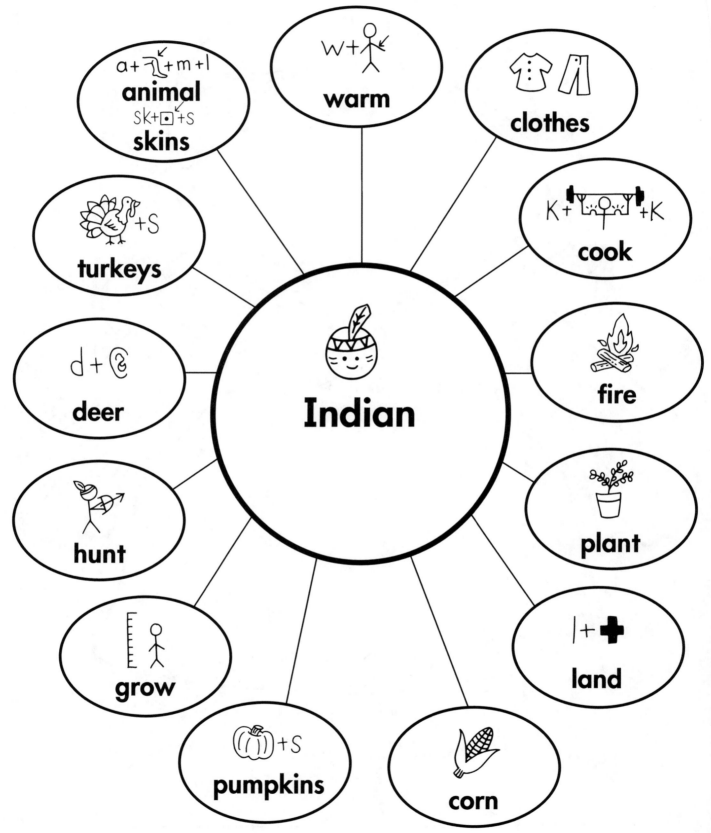

Class Book

Directions: Use words from your Picture Dictionary and around the room to help you complete the sentences. Draw a picture to go with your sentences.

I saw a _____ Indian.

He looked _____,

_____, and _____.

He had a _____ and

a _____.

By _____

Sequence Story

Directions: Color the pictures and cut them out. Glue the picture cards in order in the numbered boxes to show the sequence of the events in the Indian's day. Use the picture cards to write a story on another piece of paper. Use your Picture Dictionary and the Sequence Story Pocket Chart Words to help you.

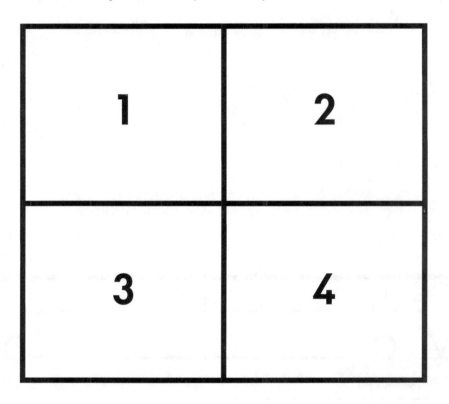

Rebus Writing • Fall © 2004 Creative Teaching Press

Pilgrims

+S

The activities in this theme emphasize the use of describing words and sequence of events. Additional vocabulary is introduced to promote descriptive and seasonal writing related to Thanksgiving.

READ-ALOUDS

If You Sailed on the Mayflower in 1620
by Ann McGovern
(SCHOLASTIC)

Oh, What a Thanksgiving!
by Steven Kroll
(SCHOLASTIC)

The Pilgrims' First Thanksgiving
by Ann McGovern
(SCHOLASTIC)

Sarah Morton's Day: A Day in the Life of a Pilgrim Girl
by Kate Waters
(SCHOLASTIC)

Three Young Pilgrims
by Cheryl Harness
(ALADDIN)

PICTURE DICTIONARY WORDS

Pilgrim
ocean
Mayflower
America
strong
brave
lived
build
houses
learn
plant
together

POCKET CHART WORDS

Descriptive Story	**Sequence Story**
black and white clothes	England
black hat	freedom
buckle	Plymouth Rock
white cap	wood
apron	vegetables
wooden shoes	fire

EMPHASIZE THESE HAVE-TO WORDS IN THIS THEME:

"K"+m

came
(/k/ + "A" + /m/)

here

d + 👻°°

do
(/d/ + the ghost sound)

don't

work

SENTENCE SQUARES SENTENCES

The Pilgrims were brave and friendly.
The Pilgrims learned to plant.
They had to build houses.
They had to live together with the Indians.
The Pilgrims learned to live in America.

SEQUENCE STORY PROMPT

Explain what it was like for the Pilgrims when they first came to America.

Picture Dictionary Words

Directions: Read each word. Cut out the picture cards and glue them in your Picture Dictionary.

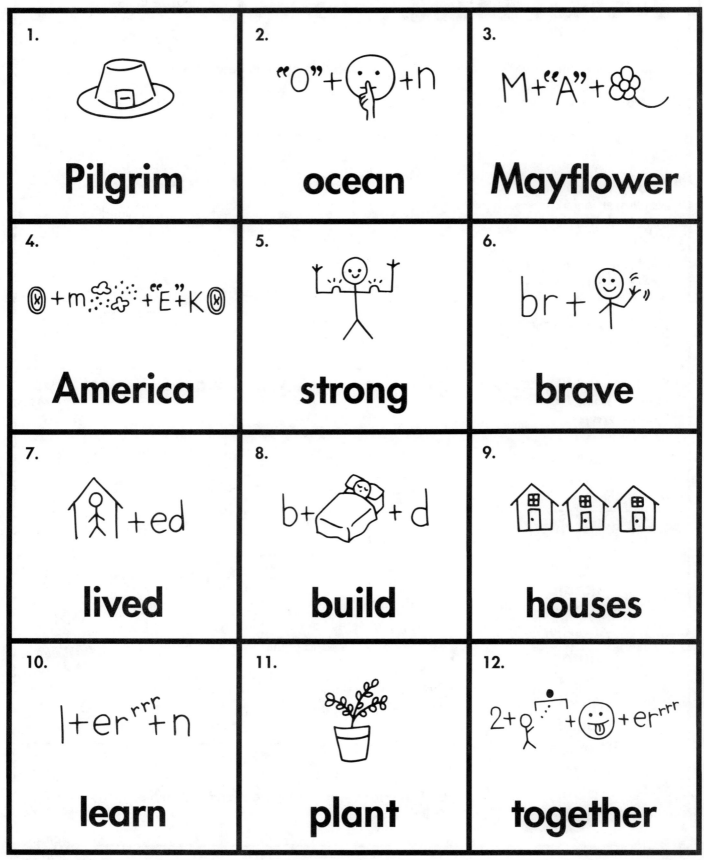

1. Pilgrim

2. ocean

3. Mayflower

4. America

5. strong

6. brave

7. lived

8. build

9. houses

10. learn

11. plant

12. together

Rebus Writing • Fall © 2004 Creative Teaching Press

Pocket Chart Words

Descriptive Story (Use with Let's Create It on page 123)

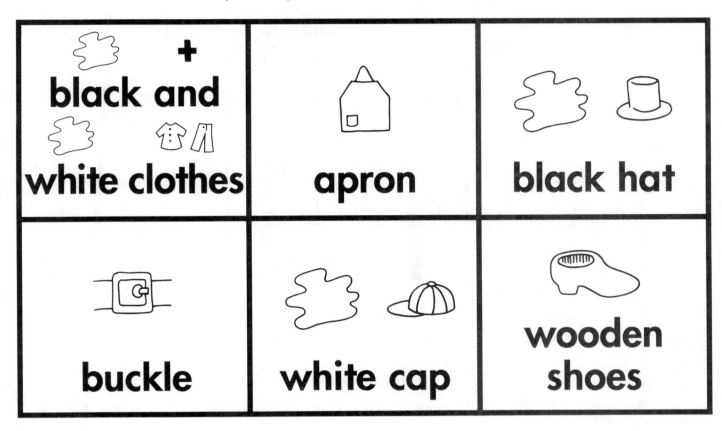

Sequence Story (Use with Sequence Story on page 127)

Word Hunt

Directions: Use your Picture Dictionary to help you find the word that goes with each picture. Write the correct word below each picture. Complete the special sentence at the bottom of the page.

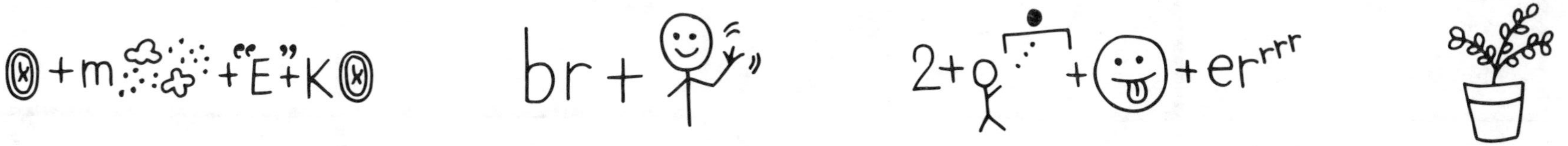

$b + d$

$lter^{rrr} + n$

$"O" + \bigodot + n$

$M + "A" + \text{❀}$

$\bigotimes + m\text{❀} + "E" + k\bigotimes$

$br + \text{☺}$

$2 + \text{☺} + er^{rrr}$

$br + \text{☺}$

$+$

was

Rebus Writing • Fall © 2004 Creative Teaching Press

Secret Sentence Booklet

Directions: Write the correct word under each rebus picture.

"K"+m

 + S

came

M+"A"+ (flower)

1

☺ + "A"

2

They had

b+d

Rebus Writing • Fall © 2004 Creative Teaching Press

2

Secret Sentence Booklet

Directions: Write the correct word under each rebus picture.

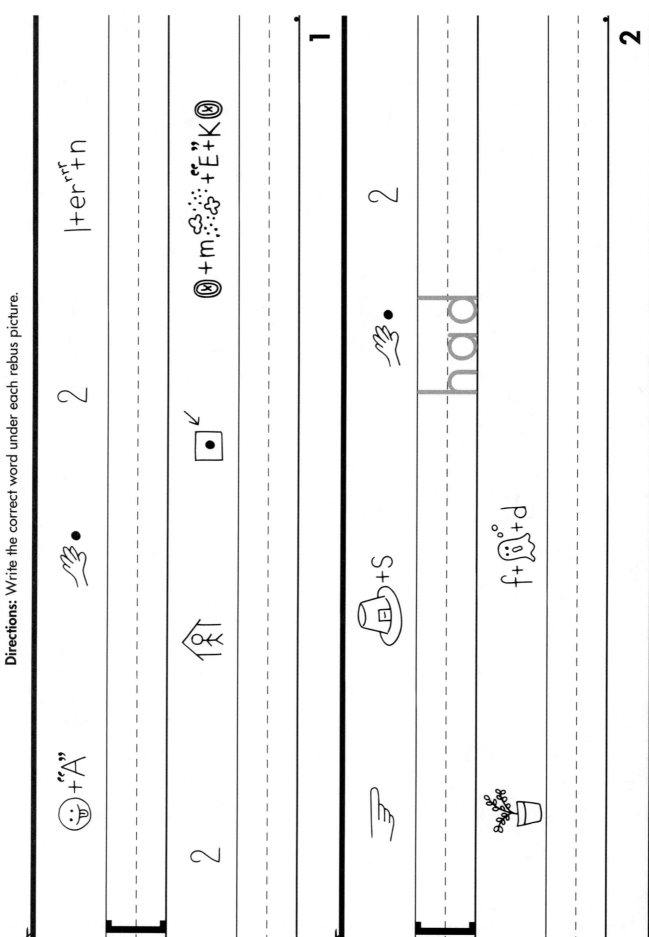

Rebus Writing • Fall © 2004 Creative Teaching Press

Bubble Writing

Directions: Write the correct word in each bubble. Use these words to complete the sentences at the bottom of the page.

Connect a Sentence

Directions: Read the phrase in the center bubble. Add words from the connecting bubbles to the phrase to make a sentence. Use additional words to create more sentences. Write the sentences on a separate piece of paper.

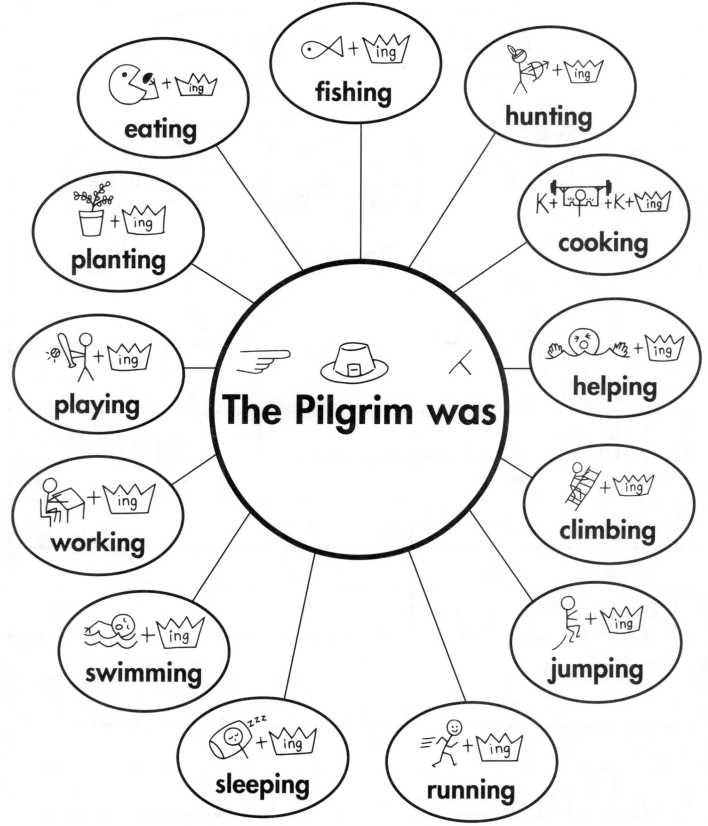

Sentence Squares

Directions: Read the word cards. Cut apart the cards and mix them up. Make sure that the words are face up. Use the word cards to make sentences.

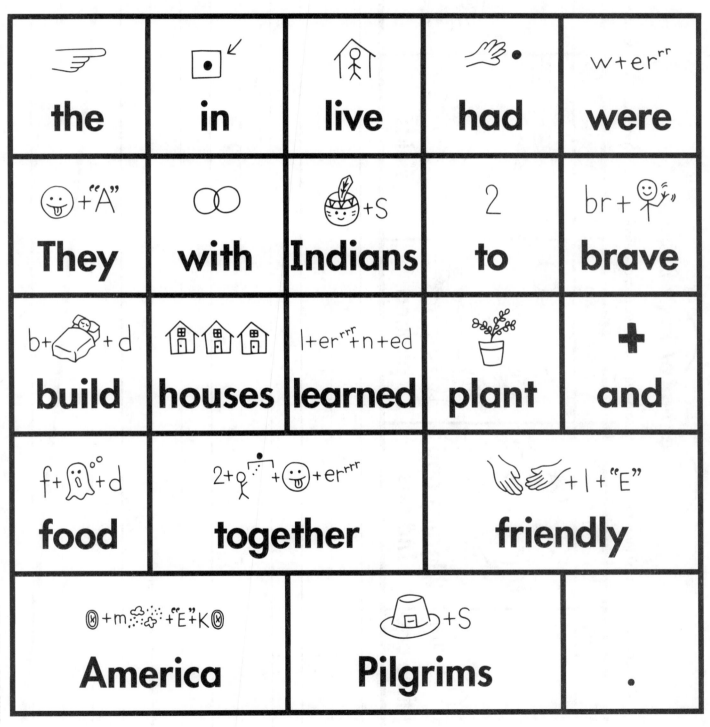

Sentence/Story Builder

Directions: Use the pictures to help you write a sentence or story that describes **who**, **what**, **when**, **where**, and **why**.

When	Who	Is Doing What	Where	Why
 A long time ago	Pilgrims and Indians	planted	fields	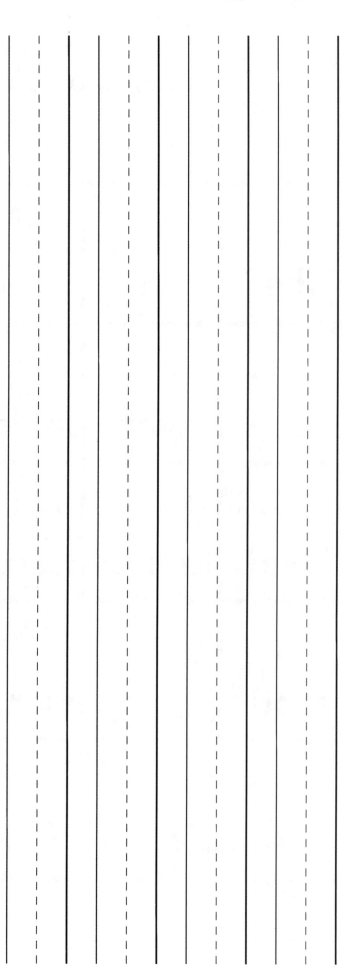 feast

Rebus Writing • Fall © 2004 Creative Teaching Press

Name_____

Story Box

Directions: Use the picture box ideas to write a story.

| **Characters** | **Setting** |
| Pilgrims | ocean |

1 Mayflower

2 Plymouth Rock

3 living together

_____

- - - - - - - - - - - - - - - - - - -

_____

_____

- - - - - - - - - - - - - - - - - - -

_____

_____

- - - - - - - - - - - - - - - - - - -

_____

Backward Story

Directions: Read the ending of the story and then tell what might have happened at the beginning and in the middle of the story.

┌───┐
│ Q U E S T I O N S   F O R   P R O M P T I N G   │
│   │
│   • When and how did the Pilgrims and Indians meet?   │
│   • How and why did they help each other?   │
└───┘

_____

- -

_____

- -

_____

- -

_____

- -

_____

☺+●+s   +   ☞   +s   **+**   +s   "B"+"K"+m

That's how the Indians and Pilgrims became

+s

friends.

Let's Create It

MATERIALS

✓ white or tan paper

✓ coffee can lid

✓ scissors

✓ crayons or markers

✓ glue

✓ writing paper

✓ Descriptive Story Pocket Chart Words reproducible (page 113)

STEP 1 Place the coffee lid on the white or tan paper and trace around it to make a circle. Cut out the circle. Choose either the pilgrim boy or pilgrim girl hat and hair to cut out. Color the hat and hair and glue it to the top part of the circle. Draw features on the circle to create a face.

STEP 2 Write a story on a piece of writing paper that tells about Pilgrims. Use your Picture Dictionary and the pocket chart words to help you.

Pilgrim Boy and Girl

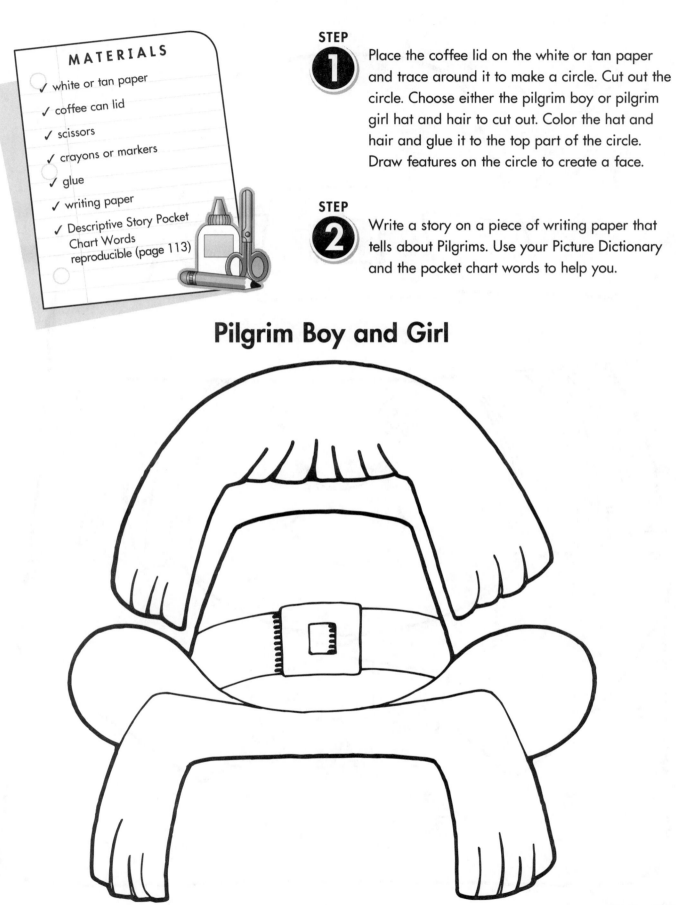

Shape Book

Directions: Color your cover. Cut out the cover and writing paper to create a shape book.

Rebus Writing • Fall © 2004 Creative Teaching Press

Word Web

Directions: Use the words on the word web to help you write a story.

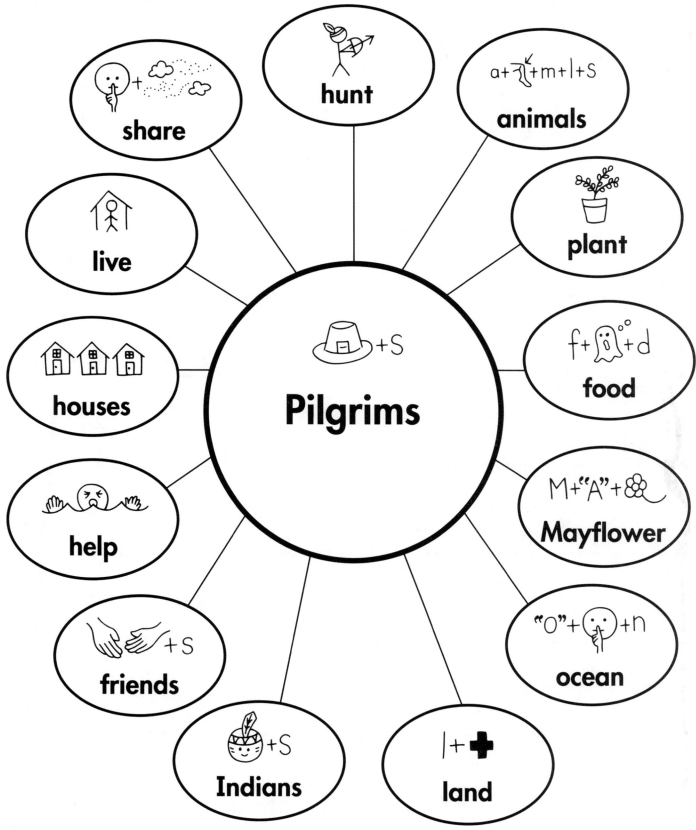

Class Book

Directions: Use words from your Picture Dictionary and around the room to help you complete the sentences. Draw a picture to go with your sentences.

I'm a little _____.

I'm _____ and

_____ and

_____.

I like to _____.

By _____

Rebus Writing • Fall © 2004 Creative Teaching Press

Sequence Story

Directions: Color the pictures and cut them out. Glue the picture cards in order in the numbered boxes to show the sequence of the pilgrim's journey to America. Use the picture cards to write a story on another piece of paper. Use your Picture Dictionary and the Sequence Story Pocket Chart Words to help you.

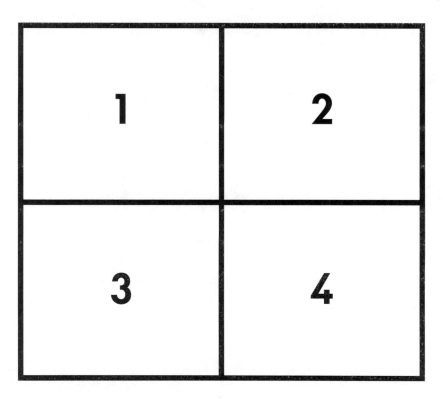